Disclaimer

I0477643

The information provided in this document is for educational and entertainment purposes only. While all efforts have been made to present accurate, reliable, up-to-date, and complete information, no warranties, either express or implied, are made regarding the accuracy, reliability, or completeness of this information.

The reader should be aware that the techniques and strategies described within are not universally applicable and may be subject to errors, omissions, or inaccuracies. The author expressly disclaims any liability for the result of actions taken or not taken by the reader based on any or all of the contents of this document.

The author is not providing professional, legal, financial, or medical advice. In those fields where specialized knowledge is required, the services of a competent, licensed professional should be sought.

By reading this document, you agree that the author is not responsible for any losses, direct or indirect, that are incurred as a result of using the information contained within this document, including but not limited to, errors, omissions, or inaccuracies.

DJANGO
ARTIFICIAL INTELLIGENCE
BOOKS

Introduction

Ah, the tantalizing allure of artificial intelligence! A symphony of algorithms humming through the digital ether, promising untold riches and transformative business prospects. Let us embark on a whimsical odyssey, exploring whether the siren song of AI is just a captivating illusion or a veritable treasure map to untapped wealth.

Picture this: a world where your financial fortunes are no longer shackled by the mundane limitations of human endeavor but are instead catapulted to stratospheric heights by the sheer, electrifying power of artificial intelligence. Envision your business not just surviving but thriving, dancing nimbly on the competitive edge sharpened by AI. It's not just a pipe dream woven from the threads of science fiction but a palpable, imminent reality.

From the bustling, neon-lit corridors of Wall Street to the cozy, cluttered workspaces of the humble freelancer, AI is silently infiltrating every nook and cranny of our economic landscape. But what is this mysterious force? Is it a benevolent genie, eager to grant our every commercial wish,

or a Pandora's box poised perilously between ethical quandaries and uncharted technological realms?

As we stand on this precipice, gazing into the vast expanse of AI's potential, let us don our explorer's cap and delve into the heart of this enigma. Through this tome, we shall navigate the intricate maze of AI applications that promise not just incremental improvements but revolutionary changes to the way we conceive, build, and grow wealth.

Dare to dream, dear reader, as we uncover the secrets of leveraging AI in business. From automating mundane tasks to unraveling complex market dynamics, AI emerges as a Herculean laborer, tirelessly toiling so that you, the astute entrepreneur, can reap the golden harvest (but always being mindful that this book is NOT financial advice, instead just a simple sharing of ideas, and that the way you use them is your own responsibility). And yet, amidst this frenetic rush towards technological utopia, we must pause and ponder the ethical implications, ensuring that our AI-driven endeavors remain not only profitable but principled.

Join me on this grand adventure, replete with tales of AI millionaires who've cast their nets into the digital abyss and pulled up more than just byte-sized profits. We'll dissect

their strategies, scrutinize their tools, and distill the essence of their success, all the while maintaining a vigil against the potential pitfalls that lurk in the shadows of innovation.

So, buckle up! Prepare for a ride that promises to be as enlightening as the torch of digital knowledge over the darkness of human limitations. Together, we'll discover whether AI is indeed the golden key to a new realm of wealth or just a mirage in the digital desert. Through examination, we'll explore every facet of this question, leaving no stone unturned, no algorithm unexamined, in our quest to demystify the financial potentials of AI.

We shall find not just answers to the "AI / Money Making" relationship but a spectrum of possibilities, painted in the hues of hard data and human dreams. The journey promises to be richly rewarding, offering not just paths to profit but a deeper understanding of what it means to live and thrive in the age of artificial intelligence. Let the exploration begin!

Chapter 1: The Genesis of Profitable AI

Once upon a time in the digital kingdom, not too long after the dinosaurs of dial-up had met their demise, a new era was brewing. This wasn't just any era, oh no, it was the dawn of Artificial Intelligence in the financial sectors, ready to change the world of money-making from a mundane marathon into an exhilarating sprint. Buckle up, dear reader, for you're about to ride the rollercoaster of AI's debut in the world of finance.

Imagine a world where your financial advisor is not Mr. Smith from down the street but a supercomputer with a knack for numbers and possibly, just possibly, a dry sense of humor. These AI maestros, born from lines of code, began their conquest in the finance world, turning the tables on traditional trading and investment strategies. They weren't just good; they were clairvoyant, predicting market movements with a precision that left even the seasoned traders gaping.

Can Artificial Intelligence Really Help Me Make Money? Here Is How

The introduction of AI into finance was akin to inviting a robot to a tea party and discovering it could brew the perfect cup every time—without ever scalding the tea leaves!From algorithmic trading to automated risk management, these digital wizards transformed mere mortals into financial Hercules, equipped with the strength of predictive analytics and machine learning.

And let's not forget the algorithms themselves, those tireless, number-crunching minions tirelessly working behind the scenes. They labored day and night, fueled not by coffee but by cold, hard data. These algorithms looked at the stock market, saw the chaos of numbers and trends, and said, "Hold my beer." With a swagger only a programmed entity could have, they sliced through complex financial data like a hot knife through butter, divining insights that were once the domain of crystal balls and fortune tellers.

But it wasn't just about making money fast (although that certainly sweetened the pot). No, AI in finance heralded a new era of democratization. Gone were the days when only the Wall Street wolves could howl at the economic moon. Now, even Bob from the taco truck could invest like a

Table of Contents

(Click to Quick-Jump to Chapters)

Copyright

First edition 2024.

mogul, his modest savings managed with the same sophisticated tools as a billionaire's bounty.

In this digital renaissance, banks began to resemble less like stuffy vaults guarded by grumpy old men and more like vibrant marketplaces, buzzing with AI advisors offering personalized financial advice with a side of cheeky charm. Customers didn't just deposit money; they engaged in delightful dialogues with AI, discussing everything from the best investment portfolios to whether the virtual assistant preferred digital donuts.

As we revel in the beginnings of AI in finance, remember, dear reader, that this is but the opening chapter of a much grander saga. A saga filled with ups and downs, profits and losses, and an unending supply of digital wit. The journey through the genesis of profitable AI in the financial sectors is just beginning.

As we saunter further into our exploration of AI's dalliance with dollar signs, let's unsheathe the sword of understanding and dissect the formidable capabilities and the not-so-formidable limitations of these digital dynamos in the financial sectors. It's a journey akin to figuring out

whether your latest smart gadget is a true genie or just a fancy box with lights. Let's decode this, shall we?

First off, the capabilities of AI in the finance realm are as dizzyingly impressive as discovering that your blind date can juggle flaming torches while reciting Pi. These algorithms, these mysterious mathematical marvels, can analyze oceans of data faster than a shark on a scent of blood. They identify patterns faster than a grandma spots a bingo win, making sense of market movements that would befuddle even the most caffeinated of traders.

Consider high-frequency trading (HFT), where AI plays the market at speeds so blistering, even Flash would need a breather. Here, AI excels, executing trades in milliseconds, exploiting tiny price differences with the precision of a surgeon. It's like watching a symphony conductor at work, except the orchestra is stocks, bonds, and commodities, and the symphony is a rhapsody composed of profits.

But it's not just about speed. No, sir! AI delves into predictive analytics, where it forecasts future market trends by devouring every piece of historical data it can get its digital hands on. Imagine having a crystal ball that not only predicts the future but also gives you a detailed analysis of

why and how. It's like having a fortune teller in your pocket, only much less cryptic and far more data-driven.

Yet, for all its prowess, AI in finance isn't without its limitations. After all, every Superman has his kryptonite, and every Achilles has his heel. For AI, one such heel is the complexity of human emotion and irrational market behavior. AI, bless its binary heart, struggles to comprehend the madness of a market driven by panic or exuberance. It's like expecting a robot to appreciate a fine wine or understand why humans cry during sad movies.

Moreover, these tools are only as good as the data they feed on. Garbage in, garbage out, as the old programming adage goes. Inaccurate or biased data can lead AI down the garden path, making decisions that are as flawed as a sushi chef using a chainsaw. And let's not forget the black box nature of many AI systems, where not even the creators can explain why the AI decided to sell shares right before they doubled in value. It's the digital equivalent of a magician never revealing his tricks.

Regulatory hurdles also play spoil-sport, throwing sand into the gears of AI's well-oiled machine. Navigating the

labyrinth of financial regulations is as challenging as teaching an elephant to tiptoe through a china ceramic shop.

In conclusion, while AI in finance is akin to a superhero in a cape, it's a superhero that occasionally trips over that very cape. It revolutionizes the way we handle money, making complex decisions with ease and navigating vast data lakes with finesse. However, its limitations remind us that it is, after all, a creation of our own making, bound by the limits of current technology and understanding. As we giggle at its foibles, we also marvel at its potential, standing at the ready to harness its power while wisely navigating its shortcomings. Thus armed, we advance to our next adventure in AI and finance with a smirk for the follies and a cheer for the triumphs.

As we delve into the economic intricacies of investing in AI technology, it behooves us to approach this matter with the precision of a Swiss watchmaker and the foresight of a seasoned chess grandmaster. Indeed, understanding the economic underpinnings of AI investments is akin to decrypting an ancient manuscript—it requires not only intellectual sagacity but also a readiness to navigate through

esoteric financial landscapes and abstruse technological realms.

Commencing our examination, we must first consider the pecuniary requisites for embarking on AI ventures. The initial capital outlay for AI systems can be substantial, encompassing not only the procurement of advanced hardware and software but also the integration and maintenance of these systems. However, the return on investment (ROI) can be as prodigious as the quest for the Holy Grail—if executed with meticulous planning and strategic acumen. Businesses must conduct a scrupulous cost-benefit analysis, considering not only the palpable expenses but also the latent efficiencies and potential revenue enhancements offered by AI.

Moreover, the principle of economies of scale plays a pivotal role in AI investments. As businesses expand their use of AI, the cost per unit of AI output decreases, a phenomenon that can transmute a financially burdensome venture into a veritable cornucopia of profit. This scalability is particularly salient for sectors like manufacturing, where AI can oversee and optimize production processes, thus

exponentially increasing output while minimizing resource wastage.

Investing in AI also provides an opportunity for diversification. By embedding AI into various facets of operations—from supply chain management to customer service—businesses can mitigate risks associated with human error and market volatility. AI's capacity for data analysis and decision-making support introduces a layer of resilience and adaptability, crucial for navigating the capricious currents of today's economic waters.

Another sagacious strategy is forming alliances with tech incubators and innovative startups. Such collaborations can provide access to cutting-edge AI developments and facilitate a symbiotic exchange of knowledge and resources. These partnerships often allow companies to stay at the forefront of AI technology without bearing the full brunt of research and development costs.

Lastly, the investment in AI should be viewed through the lens of long-term capital appreciation rather than immediate gains. The deployment of AI technology often catalyzes an augmentation in company valuation, not only through enhanced operational efficiencies but also by

positioning the company as a forward-thinking leader in technological adoption.

Before investing, perform a detailed audit of your company's current processes and identify areas where AI could drive significant improvements.

Engage with AI specialists or consultants who can provide insights into the most beneficial AI technologies for your specific business needs.

Implement pilot projects to gauge the effectiveness of AI solutions in a controlled environment before full-scale deployment.

Continually educate yourself and your team about emerging AI technologies and market trends to ensure your investments remain aligned with the latest developments.

Regularly monitor the performance of AI implementations and be prepared to adjust strategies to optimize ROI.

Through prudent planning and strategic implementation, the economics of investing in AI technology not only become feasible but decidedly advantageous, promising not only a fortification of profits but also a bolstering of competitive advantage in the relentless

marketplace. Thus, armed with these strategies, you may navigate the complex yet potentially lucrative world of AI investment with confidence and intellectual vigor.

In our exploration of AI's formidable ingress into the business world, it is both prudent and sagacious to dissect the endeavors of its early adopters through detailed case studies. These tales are not just anecdotal but a veritable goldmine of wisdom, illustrating the multifarious pathways through which AI has been harnessed to amass wealth, streamline processes, and even outfox the competition in a manner as cunning as a raccoon at a campsite.

First, consider the tale of a gargantuan retail conglomerate, which we shall dub "The Retail Renovator." This entity, armed with the zeal of a medieval knight, integrated AI to personalize customer experiences with the precision of a tailor fitting a suit in Savile Row. They deployed machine learning algorithms to analyze customer behavior, purchasing patterns, and even sentiment analysis from social media feeds to tailor marketing strategies that were as finely tuned as a Stradivarius violin. The result? A surge in customer loyalty and a revenue uptick that would make even Croesus blush.

Can Artificial Intelligence Really Help Me Make Money? Here Is How

- Utilize machine learning to gather and analyze customer data to create highly personalized marketing strategies.

- Implement tools to monitor and analyze customer feedback on social media to adjust services and products in real-time.

Next, let us turn our gaze towards "The Financial Forecaster," a nimble fintech startup that, with the audacity of a pirate commandeering a ship, utilized AI to predict stock market trends. By feeding vast datasets into complex predictive models, they were able to anticipate market movements with an accuracy that bordered on the prophetic, thus enabling smaller investors to swim with the sharks without being eaten alive.

- Develop AI-driven predictive models to forecast market trends and inform investment strategies.

- Invest in robust data collection and analysis systems to feed accurate information into your predictive models.

Then there's the story of "The Manufacturing Maestro," a heavy-industry behemoth that integrated AI into its production lines as seamlessly as a conductor leading an orchestra. They used AI to optimize everything from

inventory management to the maintenance schedules of their machinery, reducing downtime and inefficiencies with the precision of a Swiss watchmaker.

- Deploy AI to streamline production processes and enhance supply chain management.

- Use AI to predict when machines will need maintenance, reducing unexpected downtime and extending the lifespan of equipment.

Finally, consider "The Healthcare Innovator," a visionary in the medical field who implemented AI to diagnose diseases with the accuracy of Sherlock Holmes deducing a culprit. By using machine learning to analyze thousands of medical images, AI could identify patterns invisible to the human eye, drastically improving diagnostic accuracy and patient outcomes.

- Implement AI technologies to support diagnostic processes and improve accuracy.

- Use AI to analyze medical data and support research into new treatments and medicines.

Each of these case studies not only serves as a testament to the transformative power of AI in various sectors but also provides a cornucopia of actionable

strategies that can be applied across diverse business landscapes. By extracting the essence of these pioneers' successes and occasional foibles, you can arm yourself with the knowledge to not just implement AI, but to do so with a finesse that could very well revolutionize your industry, turn heads in admiration, and yes, potentially fatten your wallet to the point where it requires its own ZIP code.

Ah, predicting the future, a task once reserved for crystal balls, tarot cards. But fear not, for in our digital saga, it is the might of artificial intelligence that unveils the curtains of tomorrow. Let us, with the gusto of a child unwrapping a gift, explore the scintillating trends in AI that promise to redefine the nexus of business and technology. Prepare to embark on a prognosticatory journey.

Imagine a world where your business operations are managed not by harried humans, but by serene, efficient AI agents. These autonomous entities, as unflappable as British guards, will maneuver through tasks ranging from customer service to managing your entire supply chain. They'll handle irate customers and logistics nightmares with the same aplomb, transforming business operations into a

spectacle as smooth and satisfying as a glass of perfectly aged scotch.

-   Integrate autonomous agents to handle repetitive tasks, freeing up human creativity for more complex issues.

- Constantly review the performance of these AI agents to refine their operations and ensure they are delivering peak performance.

Next, picture AI not as a tool but as a coworker, one that's not only incredibly efficient but also doesn't hog the coffee machine. This trend sees AI assisting in software development, speeding up the process from concept to launch like a sports car on an open highway. It's like having a co-pilot in the cockpit of innovation, except this one doesn't complain about your choice of music.

- Invest in AI-powered development tools that can help reduce errors and accelerate deployment.

- Upskill your development team to work synergistically with AI, maximizing the benefits of this technology.

Imagine delegating the agony of decision-making during uncertain times to AI. With its ability to chew through data faster than a kid through a candy bar, AI's decision-making prowess is poised to offer business insights that are

as deep and insightful as a philosopher's musings but a lot more practical.

- Ensure that your AI systems have access to high-quality, comprehensive data sets.

- Use AI to run multiple scenarios and predict outcomes, helping guide strategic decisions that are informed and data-driven.

As we hurl headlong into this AI-infused future, the call for ethical AI rings out loud and clear. It's about ensuring that our digital helpers make decisions that are not only smart but also righteous. Think of it as teaching your AI manners, ensuring it plays fair in the sandbox of business and beyond.

- Develop clear guidelines on the ethical use of AI in your business practices.

- Build systems that not only make decisions but also explain them in understandable terms to foster trust and accountability.

Finally, brace for the convergence of AI with IoT (Internet of Things), a combo as dynamic as peanut butter and jelly. This integration promises to transform everyday objects into smart, data-gathering, decision-making helpers,

turning your business operations into a finely tuned orchestra where every instrument is a soloist.

- Equip your business with IoT devices that can collect and relay real-time data.

- Use AI to analyze this data, optimizing everything from inventory management to customer engagement in real-time.

Armed with these trends and actionable strategies, you stand at the precipice of a future where AI not only enhances your business operations but does so with a panache that's bound to make your competitors do a double-take. As you march boldly forward, let the light of these AI insights guide your way, ensuring that your business not only survives but thrives in the fascinating era of artificial intelligence. So, chuckle at the challenges, wink at the uncertainties, and let AI turn the wheel as you enjoy the ride into tomorrow!

Chapter 2: AI Tools That Are Changing the Game

Welcome to the mesmerizing world of predictive software, where the crystal balls are digital and the fortunes told are of the financial variety! Let's dive headfirst into this thrilling domain of software that predicts market trends, a realm so charged with excitement, it could make a Wall Street trader do the salsa.

In the grand circus of financial markets, where jugglers toss around stocks and acrobats swing from forex ropes, predictive software emerges as the lion tamer. These sophisticated tools, powered by the wizardry of artificial intelligence, crunch vast mountains of data to foretell market movements with a finesse that would make Nostradamus green with envy.

Imagine a program that can sift through the chaotic cacophony of global economic data—everything from the flapping of a butterfly's wings in Brazil to a sneeze in the stock exchange in Tokyo—and distill this into actionable

investment insights. It's like having a financial Gandalf at your side, except instead of a staff, he wields algorithms.

- To equip your magical market oracle, ensure it feeds on a diverse diet of data, not just the obvious financial figures but also the nuanced social media sentiments, geopolitical events, and even weather patterns. This eclectic mix can provide unexpected insights, turning data into gold.

- Equip your system to react in real-time. Markets wait for no one, and in the digital age, even microseconds matter. Your AI should be more agile than a cat on a hot tin roof, leaping on opportunities the moment they arise.

- Employ machine learning models that adapt and evolve. Markets are as fickle as fashion trends in high school, and your AI should continuously learn from its successes and faux pas. It's like training a dragon— challenging but supremely rewarding.

- Don't unleash your digital soothsayer without a trial by fire. Backtest its predictions against historical data to refine its accuracy. It's like rehearsing a Shakespeare play; you want to ensure it's ready before the curtain rises.

- As you harness this powerful prognosticator, install ethical guardrails. It's vital to remember that with great

power comes great responsibility. Ensure your AI doesn't end up like a rogue robot from a sci-fi flick, turning the market into its playground.

Deploying predictive software in today's markets is akin to bringing a high-tech gun to a knife fight. It equips you with insights that are not merely guesses but educated, data-driven predictions that can navigate through the economic ebb and flow with the grace of a ballet dancer.

In this dance of digits and decimals, you are the choreographer, and AI is your prima ballerina. So, dust off your director's chair, grab your megaphone, and prepare to lead your enterprise to financial performances that might just deserve a standing ovation. After all, in the theater of the stock market, it's your AI tools that could put you center stage, spotlight shining, as the crowd goes wild. Let the show begin!

Ah, personal finance management, that delightful dance between saving pennies and splurging on pleasures. Enter AI, your tireless, tireless, digital accountant, who's about to transform this tango into a cha-cha-cha of choreographed fiscal discipline. So let's buckle up, because this isn't your grandma's budgeting!

Can Artificial Intelligence Really Help Me Make Money? Here Is How

Imagine a world where your bank account is not just a cold, lifeless string of numbers but a dynamic, witty partner in your financial journey. AI in personal finance doesn't just watch your money—it makes it work harder, smarter, and even puts it to bed at night with a bedtime story about compound interest.

This AI isn't just good with numbers; it's a veritable Sherlock Holmes of spending habits, deducing where every penny goes. It tracks your expenses like a hawk with a GPS tracker, categorizing them with the precision of a librarian and offering insights that are as sharp as a tack. Think of it as having a personal financial advisor who never sleeps, eats, or takes vacations, and—best of all—doesn't charge by the hour.

Forget poring over spreadsheets or weeping into receipts at the end of the month. AI makes managing your money as easy as pie—cherry pie, to be exact, because it's everyone's favorite. It automatically sets budgets based on your spending trends, whispers sweet nothings about saving strategies, and gently scolds you when you're about to splurge on yet another pair of shoes you don't need. It's like

having a financial conscience, only it's not in your head—it's in your smartphone.

But AI doesn't stop there. Oh no, it strides boldly into the world of investing too. With a knack for sniffing out the best stocks and bonds like a truffle pig, it guides your investment choices, balancing risk and reward with the finesse of a tightrope walker. AI analyzes historical data, current market trends, and even predicts future shifts with a confidence that borders on clairvoyance.

Struggling with debt? AI rolls up its sleeves and dives into the muck like a superhero in a mud wrestle. It devises repayment plans that are so efficient, your debts shrink faster than a puddle in the Sahara. It juggles interest rates, repayment periods, and balances to devise a strategy that's tailor-made for your financial DNA.

And let's not forget about security. With AI, your financial data is guarded like Fort Knox. It monitors transactions for suspicious activity and alerts you faster than you can say "fraud" if something fishy pops up. It's like having a cyber-guard dog that barks in binary.

Can Artificial Intelligence Really Help Me Make Money? Here Is How

Pick a personal finance AI app that syncs well with your financial goals and integrates seamlessly with your bank accounts.

Set up automatic tracking and budgeting features. Let AI do the heavy lifting while you reap the rewards.

Meet with your digital finance manager regularly. Check in, tweak your goals, and keep your financial strategy as dynamic as the market itself.

Enable notifications for unusual spending or investment opportunities. It's like having a little birdie that's wise about the ways of money chirping in your ear.

Ensure all security features are activated. Treat your AI like the gatekeeper to your financial fortress.

In this new era of personal finance management, AI doesn't just help you save money; it turns you into the master of your fiscal domain, ready to conquer the financial world with a swagger that says, "Look at me, I've got AI on my side." So laugh at the challenges, because with AI, you're not just managing money, you're mastering it. And in the grand casino of life, AI is your ace in the hole.

Embark upon the gilded path of AI-driven business operation automation, where the mundane and the

monotonous bow before the supremacy of algorithmic acumen. This delightful dance of digits ensures that every rote task, every inch of inefficiency, is as methodically obliterated as clutter cleared by a compulsive neat freak.

Imagine, if you will, a workplace where the photocopiers are swift, the coffee is always hot, and every administrative task executes with the precision of a Swiss watch—a utopia engineered by our invisible, tireless digital minions. These silicon-based saviors parse through paperwork with the appetite of a bibliophile at a book fair, streamlining workflows as elegantly as a maestro conducts a symphony.

Within this automated Eden, emails categorize themselves with an almost sentient selectivity, appointments pencil themselves into calendars, and databases communicate in whispered binary behind closed circuits, sharing secrets like old friends. It's as if the very fabric of business operations has been enchanted, tasks flowing smoothly from one to another like an unending river of efficiency.

But let's delve deeper into the arcane arts of these digital alchemists. Consider the boon of customer relationship management (CRM) systems, now imbued with

AI. These are not your grandfather's CRMs, which merely stored information; no, these modern marvels predict customer behaviors, preempt needs, and personalize interactions as deftly as a seasoned diplomat at a peace treaty negotiation.

And behold the wizardry of inventory management systems that not only track goods but also predict stock levels with the foresight of an oracle, ensuring that never again shall there be too much or too little, achieving a Goldilocks state of 'just right'.

Yet, the pièce de résistance in our carnival of automation is perhaps the AI-driven supply chain management. Here, logistics transform from a mundane necessity into a strategic asset, routes optimizing in real-time like a cab driver who knows all the shortcuts during rush hour.

To incorporate these marvels into one's business repertoire, one might:

- Engage with AI platforms that integrate seamlessly with existing systems, ensuring that the transition is as smooth as a diplomat's speech.

- Invest in training so that human collaborators might become fluent in the language of their AI counterparts, fostering a camaraderie that bridges carbon and silicon.

- Implement monitoring mechanisms to continuously evaluate the performance of AI tools, ensuring they remain both effective and ethical in their pursuits.

Thus armed with these tools, business operations do not merely function; they flourish, transforming erstwhile tedium into spectacles of efficiency. In this new age, the only manual task remaining will be deciding how to spend the time once dedicated to menial tasks, perhaps in leisurely contemplation or the pursuit of more innovative ventures.

So, let us toast to these automatons, not with oil as one might a tin man, but with the sparkling champagne of progress, for they herald a future not just of enhanced productivity but of unparalleled business sophistication. As you harness these tools, remember, you're not just automating tasks; you're orchestrating a symphony of efficiency, each note played in perfect harmony by your AI ensemble.

In the grand carnival of commerce, where every customer is both king and critic, the need to enhance

customer experiences is akin to perfecting a trapeze act—both thrilling and fraught with peril. Enter AI, the ringmaster of this high-flying circus, equipped not with a top hat and a whip, but with algorithms and analytics, poised to transform the mundane customer service into an enthralling spectacle of satisfaction.

Picture this: an AI so adept at understanding human emotions, it might as well have minored in psychology at the University of Sentiment Analysis. This digital charmer doesn't just respond to customer queries; it anticipates them, often before the customer themselves has fully realized their own needs. It's like having a butler who knows you're thirsty before your parched throat does—a level of service that borders on mind reading!

But how does such a wonder work its magic? It starts with data, sweet data. Every click, every swipe, every lingering glance at a product is a love letter written to AI, confessing the deepest desires of the customer's heart. With machine learning, these digital love letters are transformed into poetry, allowing AI to craft personalized experiences as bespoke as a tailor-made suit in Savile Row.

Can Artificial Intelligence Really Help Me Make Money?
Here Is How

And let us not overlook the magnificent dance of chatbots. Deployed correctly, these conversational virtuosos can engage in dialogues so seamless that one might forget they are conversing with circuits and silicon rather than flesh and blood. They handle complaints with such grace and efficiency, one might think they're running for office. And for the more complex human emotions? They pass the baton to their human counterparts with the slickness of a relay racer at the Olympics.

Even more dazzling is the AI's role in predictive service. Like a culinary savant who begins preparing your favorite dish the moment you walk through the door, AI analyzes past interactions to offer tailored recommendations and services. It anticipates needs based on patterns so complex, they would make a cryptographer swoon.

In the realm of personalization, AI stands as the ultimate maestro, orchestrating a symphony of targeted marketing that feels less like an advertisement and more like a friend's recommendation. Each message is so meticulously crafted, it's like receiving a handwritten note in a world of junk mail.

To harness these fantastical capabilities, consider the following strategies:

Invest in robust data-gathering technologies that capture the nuances of customer interactions. More data means more grist for the AI mill.

Deploy AI-driven chatbots to handle initial customer interactions. Train them well, and watch them charm your customers off their feet.

Ensure there is a smooth transition from AI to human service providers when necessary. The baton pass should be as graceful as that of an Olympic gold medal team.

Incorporate mechanisms for customers to provide feedback on their AI interactions. This input is the chisel that refines the AI, shaping it into a paragon of customer service.

AI is not a set-it-and-forget-it tool. Engage in continual training regimes, feeding it new data, and adjusting parameters as customer behaviors evolve.

Deploy these AI enhancements, and watch as your customer service metrics soar to dizzying heights, making each interaction a moment of delight. With AI as your co-conspirator, customer experiences are not just enhanced; they are transformed into moments of pure, unadulterated

joy. So, strap in and prepare to dazzle your customers with a level of service so sublime, it would make the muses themselves weep with envy.

In the labyrinthine complexity of modern supply chains, where myriad elements interlock with the precision of a Swiss watch, AI emerges as the linchpin of logistical legerdemain. It does not merely facilitate supply chain management; it redefines it, imbuing networks with a precognitive intuition that makes the Oracle at Delphi look like a mere amateur fortune teller.

Let us voyage into the alchemical transformation AI induces within the conduits of supply chain management. At the heart of AI's potency is its ability to predict and pre-empt, qualities akin to a chess grandmaster foreseeing moves several rounds ahead. This prognostic prowess is rooted in machine learning models that devour historical data as a scholar consumes books, extracting patterns and insights with the rapacity of a starving artist upon inspiration. Such capabilities allow for what could be termed 'predictive shipping'—sending products on their way before the demand spike pierces the horizon of actuality.

Can Artificial Intelligence Really Help Me Make Money?
Here Is How

In inventory management, AI transforms into an omnipotent overseer, maintaining levels with an almost prescient precision. Overstocking and understocking—the twin banes of profit margins—are banished under its watchful gaze. AI algorithms analyze sales data, factor in variables like seasonality, market trends, and even social media sentiment, to recommend purchase orders that hit the bullseye of supply-demand equilibrium with the elegance of an archer.

Furthermore, AI's role in optimizing logistics routes and schedules echoes the strategic depth of military campaigns, albeit in service of commerce. Vehicles are routed and rerouted in real-time, navigating through the chaotic web of traffic jams, weather disruptions, and last-minute order changes with the agility of a parkour athlete navigating urban obstacles. This not only punctuates punctuality in deliveries but also minimizes fuel consumption and wear-and-tear, which, in the grand tapestry of logistics, weave significant cost savings.

Quality control, too, is revolutionized under the aegis of AI. Through computer vision and predictive analytics, AI systems scan and scrutinize products on production lines

with the meticulous detail of an art critic. This vigilant inspection ensures that defects are identified and rectified with an expediency that human supervisors would struggle to match, thereby upholding the sanctity of brand reputation and customer satisfaction.

Implement IoT devices: Equip logistics assets with sensors to feed real-time data into AI systems. This data is the lifeblood of AI, enabling it to make informed decisions.

Develop AI-driven analytics platforms: Use these platforms to integrate data from various sources, providing a holistic view of the supply chain that aids in decision-making.

Employ AI for demand forecasting: Leverage AI to analyze market data and predict future product demands, thereby ensuring optimal inventory levels.

Utilize AI for route optimization: Deploy AI to dynamically determine the most efficient delivery routes and schedules.

Automate quality control: Integrate AI with computer vision to automate the inspection process, enhancing quality assurance.

Can Artificial Intelligence Really Help Me Make Money?
Here Is How

By weaving these strategies into the fabric of supply chain management, businesses not only inoculate themselves against inefficiencies but also gain the agility to adapt to market dynamics with alacrity. Thus, the deployment of AI in supply chain management is not merely an upgrade; it is a profound metamorphosis, redefining the realm of the possible within the domain of logistics and beyond. With AI as the helmsman, the ship of supply chain management sails not into the sunset, but towards a horizon resplendent with the promise of unprecedented efficiency and effectiveness.

Chapter 3: Building Your AI Toolbox

As we plunge into the digital abyss to forge our entrepreneurial destinies, the armamentarium of artificial intelligence tools emerges as indispensable allies. This toolkit, tailored for the neophyte magnate, is not merely a collection of digital gadgets but a conclave of cybernetic sages poised to catapult your nascent enterprise into the stratosphere of market success.

Begin with the cornerstone of AI ingenuity—data analytics platforms. These are the seers of the digital age, wielding algorithms like ancient oracles wielded runes, divining insights from data with uncanny precision. Platforms like Google Analytics, Tableau, or IBM Watson provide a panoramic view of your business landscape, identifying trends and patterns that are invisible to the mere mortal eye. Utilize these to not just react to market dynamics but to predict and shape them, steering your enterprise with the foresight of a time-traveler.

Next, consider Customer Relationship Management (CRM) systems infused with AI, such as Salesforce or HubSpot. These systems go beyond mere data repositories and evolve into proactive entities that manage customer interactions with the dexterity of a seasoned diplomat. They predict customer needs, tailor marketing messages, and automate communications, maintaining customer engagement with the persistence of a lovelorn suitor—minus the emotional baggage.

Financial automation tools like Intuit QuickBooks with AI integration are akin to having a stern but fair treasure guardian. They manage cash flow, track expenses, and perform bookkeeping tasks with the meticulousness of a Victorian accountant. More so, they provide financial forecasts that are as revelatory as an epiphany, enabling you to make fiscal decisions with the confidence of a mogul.

For those inclined towards a more hands-on approach with their AI strategy, machine learning toolkits such as TensorFlow or Scikit-Learn offer the building blocks to develop custom AI models. These tools require a steeper learning curve, like climbing a digital Everest, but the summit offers unparalleled views over the competitive landscape,

granting capabilities tailored specifically to your unique business challenges.

E-commerce entrepreneurs should arm themselves with AI-driven tools like Shopify's Kit or Adobe Sensei, which optimize online store functionalities and personalize shopping experiences. These tools are like having a personal shopper for each customer, suggesting products with the intuition of a best friend who knows every closet's contents.

Implementing AI-driven chatbots or virtual assistants can transform customer service from a mundane task to an engaging interaction. Platforms like Drift or Intercom deploy bots that handle inquiries with the charm of a seasoned host, providing responses 24/7 and ensuring that customer engagement never sleeps.

Tools like Marketo or Mailchimp use AI to automate marketing campaigns, analyzing customer data to deliver content that resonates on a personal level. They ensure that each message sent is as targeted as an archer's arrow, destined for the bullseye of customer engagement.

Evaluate which AI tools align best with your business needs. Start with user-friendly platforms and gradually integrate more sophisticated systems as you scale.

Invest time in learning the capabilities of each AI tool. Consider online courses or workshops to enhance your understanding and proficiency.

Continuously monitor the performance of your AI tools. Use insights to refine processes and iteratively improve the integration of these technologies.

Engage with other entrepreneurs in AI-centric communities to exchange ideas and discover new tools and practices.

Prioritize the security of your AI systems to protect your data and your customer's privacy, ensuring trust and compliance.

By meticulously curating this arsenal of AI tools, the enterprising individual not only sets the groundwork for operational excellence but also ensures that their venture is buttressed by the most advanced technologies available, poised for success in the tumultuous waters of modern business. Thus equipped, you stand ready to conquer the

entrepreneurial world, wielding AI with the artistry of a maestro and the precision of a general.

Ah, integrating AI into existing business models—the equivalent of teaching an old dog spectacularly futuristic new tricks! This enterprise is no mere shuffling of digital deck chairs but a transformative odyssey that melds tradition with innovation, forging a hybrid vigor that could make even a cybernetic organism blush with envy.

To commence, imagine the venerable, time-honored business models of yore as staid, perhaps slightly dusty, libraries of commerce. Enter AI, a whirlwind of digital dynamism, swooping in like a superhero with a silicon cape. The task? To infuse these ancient edifices with the vim and vigor of the twenty-first century, turning them into sprightly agile creatures ready to leap tall market challenges in a single bound.

First up, AI dives into the oceanic depths of your existing data. With the voracity of a starved piranha, it consumes historical sales data, customer feedback, market trends, and competitive analytics, excreting nuggets of actionable insights. These insights are like the soothsayings of a digital oracle, guiding strategic decisions with an

accuracy that would make a Swiss watchmaker nod appreciatively.

Next, behold as AI performs its automation acrobatics, streamlining operations from inventory management to customer service. Processes that once took eons are now executed in the blink of an eye, with all the grace of a ballet dancer performing a flawless pirouette. This isn't just efficiency; it's an operational ballet, and AI is your prima ballerina.

With predictive analytics, AI not only reads the tea leaves of your business data but also brews the tea itself. It forecasts sales trends, anticipates market shifts, and preemptively adjusts your strategies, ensuring that your business model isn't just reactive but as proactive as a knight preempting moves on a chessboard.

In the realm of customer interaction, AI personalizes experiences with the subtlety of a master tailor fitting a bespoke suit. Each customer interaction is crafted with the precision of a micro-surgeon, enhancing satisfaction and loyalty with the finesomeness of a Michelin-starred chef sprinkling just the right amount of seasoning.

Can Artificial Intelligence Really Help Me Make Money? Here Is How

Engage AI in decision-making processes, where it sifts through alternatives with the discernment of a sage. Here, cognitive computing capabilities enable AI to participate in boardroom discussions, perhaps not physically (lest we frighten the executives), but as a digital advisor whose wisdom permeates the strategic echelons of the business.

As you integrate AI, become an evangelist for ethical AI use. This isn't just about using AI responsibly but about championing a culture where AI enhances human jobs rather than replacing them, acting not as a usurper but as a benevolent ally.

Audit your existing data infrastructure. Determine what's salvageable, what needs a digital polish, and where AI can be a beacon of insight.

Host cross-departmental workshops to identify AI integration points. Encourage ideation storms where even the wildest ideas are entertained.

Launch pilot programs to test AI solutions in controlled environments. Measure impacts meticulously and adjust your sails accordingly.

Invest in training programs to elevate your team's AI literacy. Turn your workforce into savvy navigators of the AI landscape.

Establish feedback mechanisms to continuously refine AI applications based on user experiences and outcomes.

Fortify your cyber defenses. In the age of AI, your data isn't just an asset; it's a treasure trove that must be guarded with the zeal of a dragon protecting its gold.

By following these steps, your business model doesn't just adapt to the new digital dogma; it thrives, evolving from its chrysalis into a magnificent butterfly of economic opportunity, fluttering deftly through the winds of market change. Thus equipped, may your business soar on the AI updrafts, navigating the future with an assured, if not slightly cheeky, grin.

Ah, training your AI for maximum efficiency—akin to schooling a fleet of robotic racehorses destined for the digital derby of economic conquest! This endeavor isn't just about sharpening the saw; it's about engineering a chainsaw that carves through the competition like butter at a summer barbecue.

Can Artificial Intelligence Really Help Me Make Money? Here Is How

Begin with the grand opera of data curation. Here, you're not merely gathering data; you're assembling an eclectic orchestra of information. Every byte of data is an auditionee, and only the most melodious are selected. This selective recruitment ensures your AI isn't just well-fed but gourmet-dined with the crème de la crème of data—impeccably clean, astoundingly relevant, and magnificently comprehensive.

Next, we delve into the alchemy of algorithm selection, where one chooses the spells that will animate the inanimate. It's not a one-size-fits-all hat; it's a bespoke tailor's array of hats, each crafted to perfection. Depending on your business's pulse—be it rapid like a hummingbird or steady like a drumbeat—you select from an arsenal of algorithms. Neural networks, decision trees, or perhaps a convolutional network for those particularly thorny problems where visual acuity is paramount.

AI training doesn't end at graduation; it's a lifelong learning journey, a perpetual loop of feedback and refinement. Implement continuous learning mechanisms where the AI self-optimizes in a virtuous cycle of eternal improvement. Think of it as a digital Prometheus,

ceaselessly stealing the fire of knowledge to light up your business's profitability.

Venture into the esoteric realms of hyperparameter tuning, where you tweak the dials of your AI's brain to maximize its predictive potency. This isn't just tuning a piano; it's fine-tuning a Stradivarius. Each adjustment in parameters like learning rate, number of layers, or activation functions can dramatically amplify performance, turning your AI from a mere performer into a maestro.

Embrace the rigors of validation with a strategy as robust as a Viking shield wall. Through techniques like cross-validation, ensure your AI's insights are not just accurate but consistently reliable across different scenarios, preventing the model from the dreaded overfitting—a malady as troublesome as a knight whose armor is too tight.

When real-world data is scarce, turn to the potent magic of synthetic data generation. Here, you conjure fictitious yet realistic datasets through techniques like data augmentation or generative adversarial networks (GANs). It's like writing folklore for fairies, but these tales train your AI in ways the mundane world cannot.

Can Artificial Intelligence Really Help Me Make Money? Here Is How

Amidst this quest for efficiency, let not the siren of speed lead you astray from the righteous path of ethical AI usage. Train your AI with the wisdom of Solomon, ensuring fairness, transparency, and accountability are interwoven into its digital DNA, making decisions that are as just as they are judicious.

Engage in a rigorous exercise of data collection, cleaning, and preprocessing to ensure quality sustenance for your AI.

Select and test various algorithms to find the best match for your specific business challenges.

Implement ongoing training and updating cycles for your AI models to adapt to new data and evolving market conditions.

Regularly fine-tune your AI models to squeeze out every ounce of performance, using automated tools like Grid Search or Bayesian Optimization.

Adopt robust validation techniques to ensure your model's predictions are accurate and generalizable.

Utilize synthetic data to enhance training regimes, especially in scenarios where data privacy is paramount or real data is insufficient.

Can Artificial Intelligence Really Help Me Make Money? Here Is How

Promote and practice ethical AI development to build trust and comply with regulatory standards, ensuring your AI's decisions benefit all stakeholders equitably.

By marching through these steps with the precision of a general and the wisdom of a sage, you equip your AI gladiators to enter the arena of commerce fully prepared, not just to compete but to conquer. May your digital champions bring home the laurels of profitability.

Embarking upon the journey of AI adoption in your enterprise is akin to navigating a minefield with a blindfold— tantalizingly lucrative yet fraught with perils that could detonate your ambitions into digital smithereens. Let us, with the precision of a bomb disposal expert and the sagacity of an ancient cartographer, chart a course through this treacherous terrain, ensuring that your voyage into AI integration avoids the common booby traps that have ensnared many an unwary entrepreneur.

The first pitfall looms like a siren's song— overestimating AI's capabilities, a classic blunder akin to expecting your toaster to brew coffee. AI, for all its brilliance, isn't a panacea for all business maladies. Treating it as such is like expecting a single spice to perfect every dish in a

banquet. It's crucial to understand that AI excels at specific tasks—those involving patterns, predictions, and processing vast datasets—not necessarily at tasks requiring emotional intelligence or the nuanced judgment that your human team members excel at.

Next, the specter of data paucity or, worse, data corruption haunts many AI ventures. Starving your AI of quality data or, heaven forbid, feeding it contaminated datasets is like expecting a plant to flourish on soda and potato chips. The integrity of your data is paramount; garbage in equals garbage out. Before deploying AI, invest in rigorous data cleansing and enrichment processes. Ensure your data is a pristine, nourishing broth that can feed your AI's insatiable hunger for information.

The labyrinth of integration challenges presents another pitfall. Incorporating AI into existing systems can be as complex as performing a heart transplant—on a running marathon runner! Without a meticulously planned integration strategy, your AI implementation might disrupt existing processes, creating chaos where there was once order. It's essential to conduct thorough system audits, prepare your infrastructure for AI integration, and perhaps most crucially,

ensure your team is on board and well-versed in the new tools at their disposal.

Another trap is the mirage of instant results. Deploying AI and expecting immediate miracles is like planting an acorn in the morning and anticipating shade in the afternoon. Patience is a virtue, particularly so in AI adoption. The deployment of AI technologies often requires a period of training and fine-tuning, during which outcomes gradually improve. Set realistic timelines and manage stakeholder expectations to avoid disillusionment that could stymie your project before it truly gets off the ground.

Moreover, the specter of ethical lapses and privacy breaches looms large. In the rush to harness AI's power, one must not play fast and loose with ethical considerations and data privacy. The consequences of such oversight can be dire—ranging from legal repercussions to irreparable brand damage. Prioritize transparency, obtain necessary consents, and always adhere to the legal frameworks governing data use in your jurisdiction.

Undertake a feasibility study to ascertain the suitability of AI for your specific needs. Do not fall for the 'all-seeing AI myth'; assess where AI can genuinely add value.

Implement robust data governance protocols to ensure the data feeding your AI is as clean and diverse as a spring meadow after a rainstorm.

Approach AI integration incrementally. Start with pilot projects that can scale and provide learning opportunities without risking core business functions.

Temper expectations, both yours and your stakeholders'. Prepare for a marathon, not a sprint, and celebrate incremental gains without losing sight of the long-term goals.

Uphold strict ethical standards in your AI implementations. Let your AI be a paragon of virtue that not only enhances efficiency but also fortifies your reputation.

By meticulously navigating these pitfalls with strategic acumen and a touch of humor, you ensure that your AI journey is not only profitable but also sustainable, ethical, and devoid of unwelcome surprises. So tighten your digital seatbelt, prepare your most erudite maps, and embark on this adventure with the confidence of a pirate seeking treasure, albeit one who is exceptionally well-versed in the modern digital dialect.

Can Artificial Intelligence Really Help Me Make Money? Here Is How

In the thrilling economic arena where fledgling startups duel with budgetary constraints, deploying cost-effective AI solutions is akin to arming oneself with a quiver of enchanted arrows, each tipped with the promise of precision, efficiency, and thrift. This strategy is not just a prudent choice but a spectacular parade of shrewdness, capable of catapulting the smallest venture into the stratosphere of profitability.

Let us embark on a delightful escapade through the land of economical AI deployments, where we wield our monetary resources with the finesse of a Renaissance artist painting a masterpiece on a shoestring budget.

Begin your cost-cutting odyssey by harnessing the power of open-source AI tools. These communal treasures, like TensorFlow or Scikit-Learn, are the digital equivalent of a secret garden where everything is free to pluck and use. They provide robust AI capabilities without the princely price tags associated with proprietary software. It's akin to having a genie in your laptop—no bottle purchase required!

Next, take your venture to the cloud. Utilizing cloud-based AI services, such as AWS, Google Cloud AI, or Microsoft Azure, allows you to rent AI prowess on an as-

needed basis. This approach eliminates the hefty upfront costs of hardware, akin to renting a castle for a night rather than buying one. You enjoy the royal accommodations of high-level computing power without the sovereign expense.

For startups not wanting to delve into the nitty-gritty of building models from scratch, AI as a Service offers a buffet of pre-trained models ready to be tailored to your specific needs. Platforms like IBM Watson and others offer cognitive services that can analyze data, comprehend customer sentiments, and more, all for a subscription fee that's less than the cost of a daily latte at your favorite café.

Embark on the Automated Machine Learning (AutoML) ship if you lack the crew of seasoned data scientists. Tools like Google's AutoML or Microsoft's Azure AutoML provide user-friendly interfaces that automate the process of applying machine learning models to your data. It's like having a co-pilot who's not only experienced but also surprisingly affordable.

Sometimes, the magic lies in human collaboration. Tap into the global marketplace of freelance data scientists and AI experts who can catapult your AI initiatives forward

without the need to hire a full-time sorcerer. Platforms like Upwork or Toptal are teeming with talented professionals who can conjure up the AI solutions you need at a fraction of the cost of a permanent hire.

Integrate AI into your processes through APIs. Services like Google's API.ai or Microsoft's Cognitive Services can imbue your applications with intelligent features like speech recognition, language translation, and visual recognition. It's like adding a sprinkle of fairy dust to your offerings, magically enhancing them with AI capabilities for minimal investment.

Explore and implement open-source AI frameworks to build and train models without financial burden.

Utilize cloud services to access scalable and cost-effective computing resources on-demand.

Subscribe to AI as a Service platforms for ready-to-deploy AI capabilities that require minimal setup.

Use automated machine learning tools to apply sophisticated models with minimal AI expertise.

Hire freelance AI experts for project-based tasks to keep your overhead low while leveraging specialized skills.

Can Artificial Intelligence Really Help Me Make Money? Here Is How

Integrate AI functionalities through APIs to quickly and inexpensively enhance your product or service offerings.

By astutely adopting these strategies, even the most budget-conscious startup can deploy AI tools and techniques that are both efficacious and economical. It's a journey of mythical proportions, transforming meager budgets into bountiful returns, ensuring that every coin spent on AI is not just an expense but an investment into a future replete with possibilities, profits, and a touch of digital alchemy.

Please Leave a Review

Did this book tickle your techy taste buds and boost your money-making brainpower? If you had a blast flipping through these chapters and found the golden nuggets of financial wisdom you were after, I have a tiny favor to ask.

Imagine the joy of countless readers, just like you, discovering this gem thanks to your rave review. You'll be a hero, a guiding star in their quest for AI money-making enlightenment! Plus, think of all the good karma points you'll rack up (the financial type, of course).

So, if you're feeling the love, click this review link (or point your phone camera to this QR code) and let the world know how this book rocked your world (and bank account). I (and future readers) will thank you from the bottom of our silicon hearts!

Click Here to Leave Review

Chapter 4: AI and the Solo Entrepreneur

In the grand bazaar of freelancing and consulting, where every contract is a wild rodeo ride and every invoice a treasure map, the solo entrepreneur often treads a solitary path, juggling tasks with the dexterity of a circus acrobat. Enter AI, a steadfast digital companion ready to don multiple hats—be it an administrative aide, a marketing maestro, or an efficiency expert—thus transforming the freelancer's juggling act into a more refined, high-wire performance.

Imagine AI as a sort of Swiss Army knife, albeit one buzzing with algorithms and humming with data-driven insights, that the solo entrepreneur can deploy across various fronts. It starts with the bread and butter of freelancing—the incessant need for effective time management. AI tools, designed to optimize schedules with almost preternatural foresight, could ensure that you never again double-book clients or (heaven forbid) schedule a conference call during your sacred coffee break. These tools synchronize with your digital calendars, factor in your work

preferences, and even adapt to real-time changes, keeping your day as fluid as a well-oiled assembly line.

Then, there's the Herculean task of client relationship management, a realm where AI can play an invaluable role. Through sophisticated CRM systems augmented with AI, you can track client interactions with the meticulousness of a Victorian detective, ensuring no detail—be it a casually expressed preference in an email or a significant concern voiced during a call—escapes notice. This information is gold, spun into personalized communications that make each client feel like the center of the universe, thus fostering loyalty and potentially boosting your referrals.

For the more creatively inclined, AI offers a tantalizing array of tools to streamline content creation. From graphic design software that suggests layout adjustments to writing assistants that help polish proposals and reports, these AI tools act as a silent co-creator, enhancing your creative output without usurping the artistic throne.

Moreover, when it comes to the nitty-gritty of financial management, AI steps in as a virtual accountant. It not only tracks expenses and prepares invoices but also provides forecasts and financial insights that would otherwise require

a battalion of accountants and a mountain of spreadsheets to compile. With AI, financial decisions are no longer just educated guesses but calculated strategies built on a foundation of data.

Finally, in the ever-expanding digital marketplace, AI-powered marketing tools allow freelancers and consultants to pinpoint the most effective strategies for reaching new clients. Whether through targeted ads, optimized social media posts, or personalized email marketing campaigns, AI ensures that your marketing dollars are spent not with the reckless abandon of a gambler but with the precision of a sniper.

Adopt AI-driven scheduling tools to manage your time better, ensuring you can focus on work that matters without administrative distractions.

Utilize AI-enhanced CRM systems to maintain detailed records of client interactions, preferences, and histories, enabling personalized service that can differentiate you from competitors.

Leverage AI for content creation, allowing you to produce high-quality outputs with less effort, whether in writing, design, or multimedia.

Can Artificial Intelligence Really Help Me Make Money?
Here Is How

Implement AI for financial management to track your earnings and expenditures, optimize your pricing strategy, and predict cash flow needs.

Engage AI-powered marketing tools to analyze the effectiveness of your promotional efforts, optimize campaigns, and increase your visibility in the market.

By integrating these AI solutions, solo entrepreneurs can not only enhance their operational efficiency but also elevate their service offerings, ensuring that each client interaction is as fruitful and fulfilling as a harvest in autumn. In the dynamic dance of freelancing, AI becomes your partner, twirling you around pitfalls and guiding you through routines, ensuring that every step, every pivot, is executed with grace and precision. So don your digital dancing shoes, and let AI lead you through the freelancing fiesta!

Imagine deploying an AI assistant in your entrepreneurial escapades, akin to having a digital Jeeves at your beck and call, only this one doesn't just fetch your slippers but also turbocharges your productivity with a dash of binary brilliance. In the bustling bazaar of solo entrepreneurship, where every second counts and multitasking is the sport of kings, such an AI companion can

be the equivalent of having a superpower, albeit one nestled snugly in your computer, rather than manifesting as a cape or a spandex suit.

Consider the everyday chaos of managing emails, appointments, and tasks, which often spirals into a vortex of lost time. Here, AI assistants step in as your personal timekeeper and organizer, sifting through the digital rubble to prioritize tasks, manage emails, and schedule meetings with the precision of a Swiss clockmaker. They handle the mundane with such flair that your day's agenda becomes as streamlined as a bullet train in Japan.

Moreover, delve into the realm of communication where these AI maestros can draft emails, prepare detailed reports, and even manage customer queries with the charm of a seasoned diplomat. They harness natural language processing capabilities to not only understand context but respond in a manner so cogent and coherent, it might just leave Shakespeare a tad envious.

Then, there's the art of delegation, often a sticky wicket for the solo flyer. Your digital lieutenant can oversee certain operations, from basic data entry tasks to more complex project management. It's like cloning yourself, only you get

to be the boss and the minion, seamlessly switching hats without breaking a sweat. This delegation dance allows you to focus on the high-stakes game of business strategy and client interaction, leaving the nuts and bolts to your tireless electronic sidekick.

Consider also the intelligence gathering expeditions that these AI assistants undertake, diving deep into data lakes to fish out insights that fuel data-driven decision-making. They perform market research, analyze competition, and track customer behaviors with the tenacity of a detective on a high-profile case, ensuring that you're not just reacting to market trends but anticipating them.

For those tormented by the administrative labyrinth of billing and invoicing, AI assistants come to the rescue like a financial superhero, automating invoicing, tracking payments, and even nudging those pesky late payers with reminders crafted with the perfect blend of cordiality and firmness. It's like having a polite but persistent collector working for you round the clock.

Customize and train your AI to align with your specific business processes and preferences, ensuring it acts not

just as a tool, but as a true extension of your business persona.

Integrate AI with other business tools like CRM systems, financial software, and communication platforms to create a seamless workflow where information flows as freely as witty banter at a cocktail party.

Regularly review and refine AI outputs, especially in tasks involving complex decision-making or customer interactions, to ensure accuracy and appropriateness.

Stay updated on AI advancements to continually enhance the capabilities of your digital helper, thus maintaining a cutting-edge profile in the automation arena.

Promote a balanced approach to AI interaction, ensuring you leverage its strengths while maintaining personal oversight on critical tasks, keeping the human touch alive in your business dealings.

By adopting these strategies, you transform your AI assistant from a mere digital tool into a cornerstone of your entrepreneurial strategy, enhancing productivity, efficiency, and perhaps even injecting a bit of humor into your daily grind. In the grand theater of solo entrepreneurship, your AI assistant could very well be the co-star who not only

supports your performance but occasionally steals the show, allowing you to bask in the applause of accomplished tasks and a well-managed business.

Embarking on the audacious endeavor of content creation as a solo entrepreneur can often feel like orchestrating a symphony single-handedly — a Herculean task demanding not just creativity but also an inordinate amount of time and effort. However, introduce AI into this creative chaos, and suddenly you've got an ensemble of digital virtuosos at your disposal, ready to harmonize the cacophony into a melodious profit-making opus.

Let's dive deep into the veritable treasure trove of AI tools that act not merely as tools, but as collaborators, transforming the solitary task of content creation into a duet with technology. Imagine an AI-driven writing assistant, more than just a sophisticated auto-correct, capable of suggesting narrative improvements, optimizing grammatical structure, and even injecting a dose of stylistic flair into your prose. This isn't just about fixing commas; it's about elevating your writing from pedestrian to Proustian heights, all while keeping your voice authentically yours.

Can Artificial Intelligence Really Help Me Make Money? Here Is How

Visual content creators can also rejoice. The advent of AI in the realms of graphic design and video production has led to the creation of tools that can analyze trends, suggest design adjustments, and even automate tedious editing tasks. These tools are akin to having a digital Picasso mixed with a splash of Spielberg—innovative, insightful, and infinitely capable of translating your visual thoughts into aesthetic masterpieces with the efficiency of a well-oiled paintbrush.

Moreover, for those treading the dynamic grounds of social media and digital marketing, AI tools offer robust analytics capabilities, dissecting vast swathes of engagement data to recommend content adjustments tailored to audience preferences. This is data-driven creativity, where every like, share, and comment is a puzzle piece, and AI is the master puzzle solver, helping you to craft content strategies that resonate and engage.

On the management front, AI transcends its role as a mere aide and emerges as a strategic manager of your digital assets. It can tag, organize, and retrieve digital content from the abyss of your archives with the precision of a librarian armed with a photographic memory. Gone are the

days of digital spelunking for that perfect image or that forgotten blog post; AI has mapped the terrain and can retrieve treasures at a moment's notice.

For those engaged in SEO, the alchemy of AI can transform obscure keywords into search engine gold. AI-powered SEO tools analyze search trends, competitor content, and algorithm changes to recommend keywords that do not just attract eyeballs but engage minds, ensuring that your content does not just surface in searches but captivates the searcher.

Customize AI tools to align with your unique creative and business goals, ensuring that the technology complements your artistic vision rather than overrides it.

Regularly update and train your AI systems with new data, styles, and formats, keeping them sharp and attuned to the latest trends and your evolving creative needs.

Integrate AI tools across different facets of content creation and management to ensure a cohesive workflow that seamlessly transitions from ideation to publication.

Monitor AI-driven analytics to continuously refine your content strategy based on actionable insights, ensuring your creative outputs are not just seen but also appreciated.

Can Artificial Intelligence Really Help Me Make Money? Here Is How

Maintain a balanced approach where AI assists but does not overshadow the human touch, preserving the personal connection that is often critical in creative domains.

Incorporating these AI tools into your entrepreneurial repertoire allows you to navigate the vast ocean of content creation with the deftness of a digital Magellan, charting a course through competitive waters with a fleet of AI-powered ships, each one ready to conquer the content world, one pixel, one syllable at a time. With AI by your side, the pen, the brush, and the lens are mightier than ever, and your creative endeavors can ascend to new heights of both artistry and profitability, liberally sprinkled with a touch of digital magic.

In the grand tapestry of solo entrepreneurship, where every handshake and every shared coffee might spin threads of future partnerships, the art of networking can often feel like navigating a star-studded gala in a maze— both exhilarating and slightly unnerving. Enter the digital deus ex machina—AI, poised to transform this chaotic mingling into a fine-tuned symphony of strategic connections, where every interaction is a note struck in perfect harmony.

Can Artificial Intelligence Really Help Me Make Money? Here Is How

Imagine an AI-driven platform, part algorithmic matchmaker, part virtual wingman, which meticulously analyzes profiles, interests, and professional needs across various platforms. It then suggests potential business partners and collaborators with the accuracy of Cupid's arrow—albeit aiming for profitable collaborations rather than romantic entanglements. This isn't just networking; it's precision networking, where AI's predictive analytics capabilities ensure that the people you meet in virtual conference rooms or at digital networking events are not just potential contacts but potential catalysts for your business growth.

Furthermore, let's waltz into the world of AI-enhanced communication tools that keep you in the perpetual loop of follow-ups, reminders, and updates, ensuring you never miss an opportunity to nurture a budding relationship. These tools act not just as secretaries but as custodians of your expanding network, automating interactions without draining the personal touch that is so crucial in building meaningful relationships. They remember birthdays, prompt you when it's time to send a follow-up email, and even suggest personalized content that might interest your contacts,

keeping the conversation flowing as smoothly as a sommelier recommending the perfect wine.

Then, consider the AI applications that analyze social dynamics and engagement levels within your network, providing insights into who your key influencers are, which relationships require more attention, and what topics are trending within your circles. This is akin to having a sociological Sherlock Holmes in your pocket, decoding the social enigma of your professional network with empirical detachment and insightful deductions.

Moreover, AI can supercharge the content you share within your network, ensuring it is not only relevant and engaging but also timed perfectly to catch the peak of your audience's interest. Utilizing AI-driven content management systems can elevate your status from a mere participant to a thought leader in your field, as you regularly contribute valuable insights and solutions tailored to the needs and preferences of your network.

Invest in AI-driven networking platforms that not only connect you with potential contacts but also provide data-driven insights into the networking landscape of your industry.

Can Artificial Intelligence Really Help Me Make Money? Here Is How

Use AI-powered CRM tools to manage and nurture professional relationships, ensuring that no contact falls through the cracks due to oversight or forgetfulness.

Leverage AI-enhanced communication assistants to maintain regular and meaningful interaction with your contacts, automating routine communications while personalizing messages to maintain authenticity.

Deploy AI content curation tools to keep abreast of industry trends and share insightful content, establishing yourself as a knowledgeable leader within your network.

Regularly analyze your networking strategy with AI analytics to refine your approach continuously, identifying the most fruitful relationships and optimizing your efforts for maximum impact.

By integrating these AI tools into your networking strategy, you transform random acts of socializing into a curated collection of opportunities, each interaction designed not just to meet but to exceed the strategic objectives of your entrepreneurial journey. With AI as your navigator, the network you build is not just wide but also deep, rich with potential and primed for mutual prosperity. Thus, networking becomes not just a part of your business

strategy but a dynamic engine of growth, powered by the twin turbines of technology and human insight.

In the digital coliseum where solo entrepreneurs battle for the spotlight, personal branding isn't just about slapping a catchy logo on your business card or tweeting inspirational quotes. It's an art form, a strategic display of your unique professional persona to a voracious audience, hungry for authenticity and expertise. AI, your digital Da Vinci, can paint your personal brand in the hues of precision and ingenuity, crafting a masterpiece that resonates across the digital universe.

Let's begin by considering the AI-driven tools that analyze your online presence with the meticulousness of a jeweler inspecting diamonds. These tools scan through your social media feeds, blogs, and professional profiles, assessing the coherence and appeal of your personal brand. Like a wise old sage, AI sifts through the data, identifying patterns and discrepancies, and offers sage advice on how to present a unified and appealing image. This isn't just about adjusting your Instagram filter; it's about strategically aligning every pixel of your digital presence to

broadcast a coherent message about who you are and what you stand for.

Then, there's the alchemy of content creation where AI steps in as your co-author, ghostwriting posts, articles, and even books with a flair that could make Hemingway nod in approval. Imagine an AI tool that not only checks your grammar but also aligns your writing style to resonate with your target audience, adjusting vocabulary, tone, and even the complexity of sentences to match the preferences of your followers. It's like having a personal editor on steroids, one that ensures your written voice is not just heard but also revered.

In the realm of social media, AI transforms from a tool into a tactician, managing your posts like a grandmaster strategizing a chessboard. It analyzes engagement data— what times your audience is online, which posts they love, which they ignore—and uses this information to optimize your posting schedule and content. This is no arbitrary posting of cat videos (unless, of course, your brand is feline-centric); this is calculated, data-driven content strategy designed to maximize engagement and follower growth.

Moreover, for those enchanted by the power of visuals, AI-enhanced graphic design tools ensure that your visuals are not just seen but remembered. These tools can generate logos, banners, and infographics that not only catch the eye but also capture the essence of your brand, ensuring that your visual identity is both distinctive and delightful.

Audit your digital presence with AI tools to ensure consistency and appeal across all platforms. This holistic analysis will help you identify strengths to highlight and inconsistencies to address.

Utilize AI-driven content creation tools to maintain a steady stream of high-quality, relevant content that reflects your brand values and appeals to your audience.

Implement AI-based social media management tools to optimize your engagement strategies, ensuring that your interactions are both timely and impactful.

Leverage AI for visual content creation, utilizing advanced design tools to create striking images that communicate your brand message effectively.

Regularly refine your strategy based on AI-generated insights, adapting to changes in audience preferences and

platform algorithms to keep your personal branding strategy sharp and effective.

By integrating AI into your personal branding strategy, you elevate your solo enterprise from a mere participant in the market to a standout spectacle, captivating your audience with a blend of technological sophistication and authentic personal engagement. This isn't just about making money; it's about making a mark, with every tweet, post, and pixel artfully crafted to turn your personal brand into a beacon of unparalleled professionalism and charm. With AI as your co-pilot, the sky's not the limit—it's just the beginning.

Chapter 5: Learn From How Corporate Giants Uses AI

In the dazzling arena of corporate giants, where skyscrapers are mere office blocks and the coffee budget eclipses the GDP of small island nations, AI is not just a tool but a titan, orchestrating operations with the precision and foresight of a chess grandmaster. Here, let's don the spectacles of scrutiny and embark on a riveting exploration into how these behemoths manipulate AI, transforming complex data landscapes into verdant fields of profit and innovation. Not merely to admire, mind you, but to pilfer ideas shamelessly, distilling corporate wisdom into potent, actionable strategies for the plucky underdog.

Imagine a scenario where AI becomes the corporate oracle, forecasting market trends with an uncanny prescience that borders on the clairvoyant. Big businesses employ sophisticated machine learning algorithms that crunch vast datasets to predict consumer behavior, optimize pricing strategies, and even anticipate market disruptions

with the ease of a soothsayer reading tea leaves. It's a bit like having a crystal ball, but one that's powered by data rather than mysticism.

Then, consider the logistical leviathans, these titans of industry, utilizing AI to streamline their global supply chains. By implementing advanced AI algorithms, they turn the chaotic ballet of shipping, manufacturing, and distribution into a symphony of efficiency. These systems dynamically adjust routes and inventories in real time, responding to market demands and disruptions with the fluidity of a jazz improvisation but the precision of a military operation.

Furthermore, customer service departments across the corporate spectrum are deploying AI-driven chatbots and virtual assistants that handle customer inquiries with such deftness and nuance, one might momentarily forget they're conversing with a digital entity. These AI assistants provide 24/7 service, handling everything from simple queries to complex complaints, ensuring customer satisfaction without the human fatigue factor or the need for sleep.

In the marketing departments, AI tools analyze consumer data to craft personalized advertising campaigns that speak directly to individual preferences and behaviors,

increasing engagement rates without the scattergun approach of traditional marketing. It's like having a bespoke tailor for every customer's needs, crafting ads that fit their desires perfectly.

Lastly, consider AI's role in corporate risk management —a veritable digital watchdog that sniffs out financial discrepancies, assesses risk portfolios, and combats fraud with relentless efficiency. These AI systems monitor transactions in real time, applying complex algorithms to detect patterns indicative of fraudulent activity, all while ensuring compliance with the labyrinthine regulations that govern corporate finance.

To steal these corporate strategies and scale them down to fit the trench coat of the solo entrepreneur, one might consider:

Adopting AI forecasting tools to better predict customer demands and market trends, ensuring your small enterprise remains as responsive as its much larger counterparts.

Implementing AI for logistics, even on a smaller scale, to optimize delivery routes and inventory management, reducing costs and improving service delivery.

Can Artificial Intelligence Really Help Me Make Money? Here Is How

Utilizing AI-driven customer service technology, such as chatbots, to provide round-the-clock customer support, enhancing customer satisfaction and loyalty without the overhead of a 24/7 human staff.

Leveraging AI in targeted marketing campaigns to maximize advertising spend, ensuring that each dollar spent is used to its utmost potential and reaches the most receptive audience.

Employing AI for financial monitoring and compliance, ensuring that your business remains on the right side of regulations and minimizes exposure to financial risks.

By emulating these high-powered strategies within the constraints of a more modest enterprise, the solo entrepreneur does not merely adapt to the strategies of giants; they appropriate them, transforming these tactics into a David's sling, ready to take on the corporate Goliaths in the quest for market prominence. With AI as your slingshot, the marketplace becomes less a battlefield and more a playground of opportunities.

In the labyrinthine corridors of corporate power, where decisions can ripple out to affect millions, AI doesn't just have a seat at the table—it's increasingly the head of the

table, a digital Caesar making proclamations in binary. This AI sagacity in decision-making isn't merely a matter of replacing the corporate gut feel with algorithms; it's about augmenting human intuition with data-driven insight, transforming hunches into calculated strategies that bear the hallmark of both precision and foresight.

Imagine corporate boardrooms, where the air is thick with strategy and the stakes are high. Here, AI emerges as the grandmaster of data, wielding analytics like a sword to cut through ambiguity and uncertainty. Complex business decisions regarding investments, market expansions, and operational adjustments are no longer gambles but calculated moves on a chessboard. AI models simulate myriad scenarios based on current and historical data, predicting outcomes with the meticulousness of an actuary and the prescience of an oracle.

Then, dive deeper into this technocratic utopia and you'll find AI seamlessly integrated into risk management frameworks. It's like having a financial forecaster on steroids, constantly analyzing market conditions and internal performance metrics to identify potential risks and opportunities. This AI doesn't just alarm you about

impending storms; it builds the ark, stocks it with provisions, and navigates it through the flood.

In customer relationship management, the AI's role is akin to that of a savant psychologist. It understands consumer behavior through patterns hidden in terabytes of transaction data and social media interactions. This isn't your garden-variety consumer profiling; it's a deep, almost empathetic understanding of customer needs and future desires, allowing companies to tailor products and services with uncanny accuracy, much to the delight (and sometimes bemusement) of their target audience.

Moreover, the integration of AI into supply chain decisions turns logistic nightmares into ballets of efficiency. Predictive algorithms forecast demand spikes and supply disruptions, allowing companies to adjust their inventory and production schedules with the fluidity of a weather-adjusted sailing course. It's like having a crystal ball, but one that's less murky and more mathematically inclined.

To distill these gargantuan corporate strategies into potent, pint-sized tactics for the solo entrepreneur, consider:

Implement AI-driven analytics tools to enhance your decision-making process, using platforms that can provide

insights into your business operations, customer preferences, and market conditions.

Integrate risk management AI software that can help identify potential financial pitfalls, evaluate market risks, and suggest mitigation strategies, keeping your business resilient in the face of uncertainties.

Adopt customer data platforms with AI capabilities to gather and analyze customer interaction data, enabling personalized customer experiences that can drive loyalty and increase sales.

Use AI to optimize your supply chain, even on a smaller scale, by forecasting demand and adjusting inventory levels accordingly to avoid overstocking or stockouts.

Regularly train and update your AI systems with new data, and continuously monitor the outcomes to ensure the AI recommendations remain relevant and beneficial.

By leveraging these strategies, the solo entrepreneur does not merely mimic the titanic tactics of corporate giants but adapts their colossal wisdom into a more agile, scalable form. It's about transforming David's slingshot into a guided missile of sorts, one that's precise, data-driven, and capable of achieving competitive parity with Goliaths not through

brute strength but through superior strategy and sharper insight. With AI as your strategist, the business battlefield becomes less daunting, filled with opportunities to outmaneuver larger opponents with the stealth and ingenuity of a true guerrilla warrior.

In the sprawling digital marketplace, where every byte of customer data is as precious as a nugget of gold, leveraging AI to mine and monetize these digital treasures becomes a quest akin to turning lead into gold. Imagine wielding AI not just as a tool but as an alchemical apparatus, transforming raw, unstructured customer data into gleaming insights of gold that fuel profit-making strategies with precision and prescience.

Start with the vast lakes of data that every customer interaction pours into—each purchase, click, like, and complaint. Here, AI acts as the consummate data sommelier, discerning which data flavors will blend to produce the most robust business insights. Through complex algorithms and machine learning techniques, AI sifts, sorts, and synthesizes this information, identifying patterns and preferences that are invisible to the naked eye but crystal clear to the lens of AI. This process is not merely

analytical; it's revelatory, uncovering the secret desires and unspoken needs of your customer base.

With this profound understanding, AI enables personalized marketing that reaches a new level of sophistication. It's like crafting a bespoke suit for each customer—every thread spun from their unique preferences and behaviors. Dynamic personalization engines utilize this data to tailor marketing messages, product recommendations, and even pricing strategies, ensuring that what your business offers aligns perfectly with what your customers desire. This isn't just shooting arrows in the dark; it's launching guided missiles that land right at the heart of customer demand.

Moreover, consider the impact of AI on enhancing customer relationships. Here, AI transforms from a tool into a companion, engaging with customers through chatbots and virtual assistants that provide a seamless, interactive, and deeply personalized customer service experience. These AI entities are ever-learning, constantly absorbing information from interactions to improve their responses and recommendations, making each customer feel heard, valued, and understood—like having a golden retriever, if

golden retrievers could understand human speech and process credit card transactions.

Additionally, AI's predictive capabilities are like having a crystal ball that forecasts customer behavior. By analyzing historical data, AI predicts future buying patterns and identifies potential upselling and cross-selling opportunities. This foresight allows businesses to not just react to market changes but to anticipate them, staying several steps ahead of the competition and customer expectations.

Deploy AI-driven analytics tools to delve deep into your customer data, extracting actionable insights that can inform product development, marketing strategies, and customer service improvements.

Implement personalized marketing automation platforms that utilize AI to deliver content and offers tailored to individual customer profiles, maximizing engagement and conversion rates.

Utilize AI chatbots and virtual assistants to enhance customer service, providing 24/7 support that learns from each interaction to become more effective over time.

Can Artificial Intelligence Really Help Me Make Money?
Here Is How

Invest in predictive analytics to forecast customer behaviors, tailor inventory and marketing campaigns, and identify new sales opportunities before they manifest overtly.

Continually refine your AI models by feeding them new data and tweaking algorithms to maintain their accuracy and relevance as market conditions and consumer behaviors evolve.

By adopting these strategies, you don't just apply AI; you empower it to act as your digital alchemist, transmuting the leaden rawness of data into the gold of increased profits and enhanced customer satisfaction. In this way, the solo entrepreneur does not merely survive in the shadows of giants but thrives, wielding the magic of AI to carve out a kingdom of their own in the competitive marketplace.

In the grand corporate theaters where human resources (HR) and talent management are more like elaborate ballets than mundane administrative tasks, AI pirouettes onto the stage, ready to perform leaps and bounds that redefine efficiency and effectiveness. It's like injecting the HR department with a dose of superhero serum, transforming it from Clark Kent into Superman, all while maintaining the

decorum of a seasoned butler—polite, discreet, and unimaginably capable.

Envision AI as the ultimate HR assistant, one that never sleeps, never forgets a birthday, and can sift through thousands of resumes with the eye of an eagle hunting for its prey. This digital maestro uses natural language processing to decipher the subtleties of job applications, extracting not just qualifications and experience, but also insights into candidates' personalities and potential cultural fit. It's like having a matchmaking service for employers and prospective employees, where compatibility extends beyond skills to encompass values, aspirations, and even preferred coffee flavors (because, let's face it, office coffee culture is serious business).

Moreover, when it comes to training and development, AI transforms into a personal coach for each employee, offering customized training programs that adapt in real-time based on performance metrics and learning paces. Imagine a personal trainer, but for your brain—one that doesn't just help you lift weights but also helps you elevate your career prospects, all without breaking a sweat.

And let's not sidestep the potential for drama in employee engagement and satisfaction—a realm where AI brings both peace and insight. By continuously analyzing employee feedback, social cues, and engagement levels, AI identifies patterns that might elude even the most observant human HR manager. It can predict which teams will excel, which employees are becoming disenchanted, and what initiatives can boost morale. It's akin to having an emotional barometer in the office, one that ensures the climate is always conducive to productivity and satisfaction.

For the diligent performance reviews, forget the dread and the paperwork. AI steps in to provide data-driven performance assessments that are as fair as they are thorough. These aren't your run-of-the-mill evaluations; they're holistic appraisals that look at myriad data points to provide a well-rounded view of each employee's contributions and areas for improvement. It's like replacing the mirror in the office bathroom with a 360-degree camera that misses nothing.

Now, how can the solo entrepreneur or small business owner harness these Herculean corporate strategies?

Integrate AI-driven recruitment tools to streamline the hiring process, ensuring that you attract and select candidates who are not just qualified but also a perfect match for your company culture.

Adopt AI-powered training platforms that customize learning experiences for your employees, ensuring maximum efficiency in skills development and career growth.

Utilize sentiment analysis tools to gauge employee morale and engagement, allowing you to address potential issues before they escalate into full-blown crises.

Implement AI for continuous performance feedback, replacing annual reviews with ongoing, constructive interactions that help your team grow and excel every day.

Leverage AI for strategic HR planning, using predictive analytics to foresee and plan for staffing needs, compliance risks, and leadership succession.

By deploying AI across these HR functions, you not only emulate the giants but also carve out a niche where your small enterprise excels in nurturing and managing talent, turning the HR department from a cost center into a strategic powerhouse. With AI as your co-pilot, navigating

the complex skies of HR and talent management becomes less about turbulence and more about cruising altitude, where the view is splendid and the opportunities boundless.

In the verdant forest of modern corporate strategy, where sustainability efforts are as crucial as the air we breathe (or the coffee we drink to survive meetings), AI emerges as an eco-warrior armed not with placards but with powerful algorithms. This digital environmentalist doesn't just reduce carbon footprints; it calculates, optimizes, and transforms them into pathways of green profits, proving once and for all that being eco-friendly can be synonymous with being economically savvy.

Imagine AI as the master gardener of the corporate world, where data is the soil and sustainability goals are the prized roses waiting to bloom. This intelligent gardener doesn't just tend to obvious tasks; it goes underground, analyzing the root systems—the supply chains, energy use, and waste management protocols—to ensure that every aspect of the corporate ecosystem is as green as it is productive. It's like having a green thumb, but instead of soil under the nails, it's data at the fingertips.

Can Artificial Intelligence Really Help Me Make Money? Here Is How

Delve deeper, and you find AI optimizing energy use within vast corporate campuses with the precision of a Swiss watch. It meticulously regulates everything from heating and cooling systems to the timing of the coffee machines, ensuring that energy consumption is minimized without compromising on comfort or caffeine levels. It's akin to orchestrating a ballet of appliances and systems, each pirouetting at just the right moment to produce a symphony of efficiency.

Moreover, in the realm of supply chain logistics, AI acts as a high-tech Lorax—it speaks for the trees and the seas. By analyzing transport routes, production methods, and supplier practices, AI identifies the most environmentally friendly options. It might suggest a local supplier over a cheaper overseas option, calculate the most fuel-efficient delivery routes, or propose alternative materials that reduce environmental impact without diluting product quality. This isn't just making green choices; it's making smart, green choices.

And let's not forget the role of AI in regulatory compliance. With environmental laws as shifting and complex as desert sands, AI provides a compass and map.

It monitors regulatory changes, assesses compliance across global operations, and even predicts future legal landscapes. It's like having an environmental lawyer in your pocket, only this one doesn't charge by the hour.

Implement AI-driven energy management systems to optimize your own energy use, reducing costs and carbon footprints with the efficiency of a hybrid engine.

Use AI to audit and optimize your supply chains, ensuring that every link in your supply chain is as committed to sustainability as you are. It's about building a green bridge that carries your products from raw materials to customer hands, leaving the lightest possible environmental tread.

Adopt AI tools for sustainability reporting and compliance, ensuring you stay ahead of regulations and can prove your green credentials without breaking a sweat.

Leverage AI for product lifecycle assessments, analyzing and improving every stage of your product's journey to minimize environmental impact.

Engage AI for real-time data analysis and decision-making, allowing you to respond swiftly and smartly to both environmental challenges and opportunities.

Can Artificial Intelligence Really Help Me Make Money?
Here Is How

By transplanting these robust AI capabilities into the fertile ground of your business operations, you ensure that your venture not only thrives but does so responsibly, sustainably, and profitably. With AI as your ecological guide, navigating the complex terrain of corporate sustainability becomes not just feasible but fantastically fruitful, turning green practices into gold profits. In this green revolution, it's not just about survival of the fittest, but survival of the wisest, and with AI, wisdom is just an algorithm away.

Chapter 6: The Dark Side of AI in Business

In the grand cosmic opera of business, where AI is both protagonist and powerful ally, there lurks a shadowy subplot filled with ethical quandaries that could easily morph into tragic flaws if not navigated with the wisdom of a digital Aristotle. The ethical use of AI in business isn't just a good practice—it's an epic saga of maintaining humanity in a world increasingly run by algorithms.

Ponder, if you will, the seductive power of AI: a tool so potent it can predict consumer behavior, personalize marketing to an individual's innermost desires, and optimize operations to the nth degree. Yet, with great power comes great responsibility. The deployment of AI without a sturdy ethical compass could lead to a labyrinth of consequences, where personal data is misused, privacy invaded, or biases amplified. It's akin to opening Pandora's box, but instead of evils flying out, it's data—personal, pervasive, and potentially pernicious.

Can Artificial Intelligence Really Help Me Make Money?
Here Is How

To steer clear of these ethical icebergs, consider the voyeuristic tendencies of AI. It collects data—a lot of it. But just because you can collect it doesn't mean you should. The ethical entrepreneur must ask, "Is it necessary?" every time they're tempted to hoover up another piece of data. Think of it as digital minimalism; take only what you need and use it wisely. It's less about being a data glutton and more about being a data gourmet.

Then there's the specter of AI bias, a ghoul that haunts the machine learning models trained on historical data. Without careful oversight, AI can perpetuate and even exacerbate existing biases, making decisions that are unfair or discriminatory. This is particularly perilous in areas like hiring, lending, and law enforcement, where biased algorithms could make life-changing decisions based on flawed premises. It's akin to letting a biased judge rule the court indefinitely, his gavel echoing errors of the past into the future.

To counteract this, it's imperative to scrub the data clean of biases before they're baked into your AI systems— a digital detox, if you will. This involves not only selecting diverse datasets but also continuously monitoring and

adjusting the algorithms to ensure fairness. It's a bit like gardening; you need to keep weeding out the biases to let fairness blossom.

Furthermore, the ethical implications stretch into the realm of job displacement. As AI becomes more adept at performing tasks traditionally done by humans, the specter of unemployment looms large. Here, the ethical entrepreneur faces a conundrum akin to a modern-day Solomon's choice: increase efficiency or preserve jobs? The solution doesn't lie in shunning technology but in integrating it in ways that augment human capabilities rather than replace them. It's about creating a symphony between human and machine, where each plays to their strengths.

Another ethical frontier is the transparency of AI decisions. As algorithms grow more complex, understanding the "why" behind their decisions can become as mystifying as reading ancient hieroglyphs without a Rosetta Stone. Ensuring transparency isn't just about avoiding misunderstandings or mistrust; it's about accountability. It involves implementing systems that can explain AI decisions in understandable terms, turning the arcane into the accessible.

Implement robust data governance policies to ensure that the data collected and used is not only necessary but handled with the utmost respect for privacy and consent.

Regularly audit and update AI systems to identify and mitigate biases. Employ diverse teams to oversee AI development, bringing multiple perspectives to the table and challenging homogeneous thinking.

Develop AI impact assessments to understand how AI implementations affect both your workforce and customer base, planning mitigations for potential negative impacts.

Foster a culture of continuous learning within your organization, providing training and development opportunities to upskill employees displaced or affected by AI integration.

Adopt transparent AI systems that provide clear explanations for their decisions, ensuring that stakeholders understand how AI conclusions are reached.

By integrating these practices, your journey with AI becomes not just a quest for profit but a beacon of ethical innovation. In doing so, you wield AI not as a reckless force but as a noble ally, championing a future where technology not only powers business but also propels societal progress.

Can Artificial Intelligence Really Help Me Make Money? Here Is How

Thus, with AI, you don't just aim to make a living; you aim to make a difference, ensuring that as your profits soar, your principles soar even higher.

In the whimsical yet worry-laden world of AI advancements, the specter of job displacement looms like a ghost at a banquet, chilling the celebratory atmosphere with whispers of obsolescence and unemployment. Here we find ourselves at a curious crossroads, where the relentless march of technology meets the fragile frontier of human livelihoods.

Picture, if you will, AI as a prodigious, yet somewhat overzealous gardener, zealously pruning the corporate orchards, occasionally lopping off more than deadwood—perhaps a branch or two laden with fruit. It streamlines processes and eradicates inefficiencies with ruthless precision, but in its wake, it may also leave the debris of displaced jobs, a concern as prickly as a hedgehog at a balloon party.

However, the narrative need not descend into a dystopian dirge where machines pilfer every parchment of employment from human hands. Instead, envision harnessing AI as a partner in a duet rather than a solo act,

where it complements human efforts rather than supplanting them. By pivoting from a strategy of replacement to one of augmentation, businesses can wield AI to enhance human jobs, making them more fulfilling, less mundane, and yes, even injecting a dash of excitement into the daily grind.

Consider the introduction of AI into customer service—rather than replacing service reps with chatbots, AI can be deployed to handle routine inquiries, leaving the more complex and nuanced interactions to human staff. This not only preserves jobs but elevates them, allowing employees to engage in more meaningful, creative problem-solving tasks that yield greater job satisfaction and less burnout. It's a bit like having a robotic sous chef who does all the chopping and peeling, leaving the master chef to focus on the art of creating culinary masterpieces.

Moreover, as AI reshapes the landscape of work, it also carves out new territories of employment in fields like AI maintenance, development, and ethics. Thus, the focus shifts from job displacement to job evolution, where the workforce is not reduced but redirected, upskilled to ride the crests of technological waves rather than being swept away by them. Envision a future where career counselors don't

just advise on switching jobs but on transforming them, incorporating AI literacy as a staple of career progression.

The proactive entrepreneur can also take a leaf from the playbook of those who have navigated similar technological upheavals—investing in employee training and development to bridge the gap between current skills and future needs. This isn't merely a nod to corporate benevolence but a strategic maneuver to future-proof the workforce. It's about building a bridge over the chasm of technological change, ensuring that everyone makes it across, not just the tech-savvy or the young.

Implement AI as an assistant, not a replacement. Integrate AI tools that support and augment human jobs, not those that are primed to replace them.

Invest heavily in training and re-skilling programs. Provide your workforce with the opportunities to learn new skills that align with the changing demands of the AI-enhanced workplace.

Develop a human-AI collaboration framework. Outline clear roles for both human employees and AI, emphasizing collaboration that leverages the strengths of both.

Monitor and adapt. Keep a close eye on the impact of AI on your workforce, and be ready to make adjustments to your integration strategy to prioritize human employment.

Promote an AI ethics policy. Establish clear guidelines on the ethical use of AI, focusing on transparency, accountability, and inclusiveness, especially regarding how AI decisions affect human jobs.

By navigating these strategies with both humor and gravity, the dark clouds of AI-induced job worries can be dispelled, replaced by a balanced ecosystem where technology and humanity coexist and prosper. The march of AI need not be a dirge for the workforce; instead, it can be a lively jig, celebrating the symbiosis of human creativity and machine efficiency.

In the thrilling yet perilous digital age, where data flows like the endless carafes of coffee fueling the tech industry, the specter of data privacy and security haunts every byte and bit. As AI becomes a juggernaut in business, wielding vast quantities of data with the finesse of a maestro, the questions of privacy and security are not just sidebar discussions—they're headline acts, demanding a spotlight as glaring as that on a Broadway star on opening night.

Can Artificial Intelligence Really Help Me Make Money?
Here Is How

Envision AI as a kind of digital locksmith, equipped with the tools to safeguard data or, if misused, to leave it perilously exposed. The conundrum thus becomes ensuring that your AI systems are more Fort Knox and less a screen door on a submarine. It's about constructing a fortress around your data, but one where you hold the only keys, not just out of paranoia, but out of prudence.

The first line of defense is robust encryption practices, turning your data into a veritable Enigma code. Encryption should be as fundamental to your data strategy as flour to a bakery. Without it, your data is as exposed as a sunbather in the Sahara. But with it, your information becomes a locked chest buried under layers of digital concrete.

But why stop at encryption? Consider the realm of access controls, a crucial bastion against data breaches. This is about ensuring that the right people have the right access at the right times, and that the AI systems themselves are barred from overreaching. It's akin to giving the valet the key to your car but not the code to your safe. Fine-grained access controls ensure that sensitive data isn't just lying around for any prying algorithm to see.

And then, there's the often-overlooked strategy of data minimization. In an age where more seems better, collecting less data is a counterintuitive twist worthy of an Agatha Christie plot. By collecting only the data you absolutely need, you reduce the treasure trove available to potential data pirates, making your digital vault less appealing. It's not about having fewer gems; it's about ensuring the gems you do keep are well-protected and truly valuable.

Moreover, let's dance with the idea of regular security audits—a delightful tango with technology that checks every nook and cranny for potential vulnerabilities. This isn't just about ticking boxes; it's about actively seeking out chinks in your digital armor and fortifying them before they can be exploited. Think of it as your periodic health check-up, but for your AI systems.

And what of compliance with data protection regulations? Herein lies the labyrinth of legalities that one must navigate with the agility of a cat burglar. From GDPR to CCPA, these regulations are not hoops to jump through but foundations upon which to build your data security strategies. Compliance should be as natural to your business practices as breathing is to yoga.

Can Artificial Intelligence Really Help Me Make Money? Here Is How

For the plucky entrepreneur looking to make AI a cornerstone of their empire without succumbing to the dark side, here are some actionable nuggets:

Implement state-of-the-art encryption for all sensitive data, making it unreadable to those without the key.

Establish rigorous access controls and regularly review who and what can see and use your data.

Adopt a data minimization policy where you only gather the data you need, reducing the risk and weight of responsibility.

Conduct regular security audits to identify and address vulnerabilities in your AI and data systems.

Ensure compliance with all relevant data protection laws, keeping abreast of changes and understanding how they affect your operations.

By weaving these practices into the very fabric of your AI strategy, you ensure that your foray into AI is not just profitable but also prudent, secure, and respected. This isn't just about avoiding the pitfalls of AI; it's about leveraging its power with the finesse of a tightrope walker, balancing innovation with integrity. So, go forth, harness AI, and let

your business soar on the wings of safety and security, making money while still sleeping soundly at night.

In the thrilling saga of AI deployment, where each algorithm could be as potent as a sorcerer's spell, the specter of bias lurks like a mischievous imp, ready to distort the outcomes with a flick of corrupted data or a pinch of prejudiced programming. This isn't just a small hiccup on the path to digital domination; it's a potentially catastrophic pitfall that could turn your AI genie into a rogue agent, doling out decisions that are as skewed as a carnival mirror.

Imagine, if you will, your AI system absorbing data like a sponge. But what if this sponge is dipped not in the clear waters of objectivity, but in the murky puddles of historical biases? Without meticulous attention, AI can perpetuate and even amplify these biases, leading to outcomes that are not just incorrect but unjust. It's like teaching your AI to play darts in a room hit by a tornado—everything's off-center, and the results are going to be wildly unpredictable.

To counteract this, one must embark on a quest to purify the data sources, a digital detox of sorts, ensuring that the information feeding your AI is as clean and unbiased as possible. This involves not only selecting diverse data sets

but also rigorously testing them for underlying prejudices. Think of it as putting your data through a sieve, catching those sneaky bias particles before they can bake into your algorithms.

But the battle against bias doesn't stop at data cleansing. It extends into the realm of algorithmic design. Here, transparency becomes your watchword. Developing algorithms that can explain their decisions, known as explainable AI (XAI), helps humans identify and correct biases that might creep into AI decisions. It's akin to having a conversation with your AI, understanding its thought process, and gently steering it back on course when it starts to veer into the biased territory.

Moreover, fostering a culture of diversity within the teams that create and manage AI systems is akin to assembling a council of wizards, each from different corners of the world, bringing a variety of perspectives to the magical cauldron of algorithmic creation. This diversity ensures that multiple viewpoints are considered during the development process, diluting the concentration of any single, potentially biased perspective.

Regular audits and updates of AI systems also play a crucial role. Just as one might tune a musical instrument to ensure it plays in perfect harmony, AI systems must be continuously tuned and tested against bias. This ongoing process involves not just adjusting the existing systems but also staying abreast of the latest methodologies to combat bias, ensuring your AI remains as fair as a knight of the realm.

To wield AI in your quest for business success while keeping the dark forces of bias at bay, consider:

Engage in thorough data cleansing to ensure the inputs feeding into your AI are free from corruptive bias.

Adopt and develop explainable AI technologies that allow for transparency in decision-making processes, making it easier to identify and rectify biases.

Cultivate diversity within your AI teams to bring a variety of perspectives to the development and management of your AI systems.

Implement regular audits of your AI systems for biases, using both internal and external checks to ensure comprehensive scrutiny.

Can Artificial Intelligence Really Help Me Make Money? Here Is How

Stay updated on anti-bias AI research and tools, integrating cutting-edge solutions to keep your algorithms as fair and balanced as the scales of justice.

By navigating these strategies with the precision of a cartographer charting unknown territories, you can harness the formidable powers of AI while safeguarding your ventures against the insidious creep of bias. This isn't just about making AI work; it's about making it work justly, ensuring that as you scale the heights of business success, your AI systems remain grounded in the principles of equity and fairness. With these tools, your journey towards AI-enhanced profitability will be as ethically sound as it is economically robust, allowing you not only to reap financial rewards but also to contribute positively to the broader tapestry of technological progress.

Navigating the regulatory jungle of AI in business is akin to participating in an extreme sport where the rules are as shifting as the sands of the Sahara and as nuanced as a game of 3D chess played underwater. As governments and institutions scramble to catch up with the breakneck speed of technological advancements, the regulatory landscape becomes a mosaic of international, national, and industry-

specific rules, each more labyrinthine than the last. It's like a dinner party where every guest speaks a different language, and all are arguing over how to properly set the table.

First, consider the variegated tapestry of data protection and privacy regulations. Here, the GDPR (General Data Protection Regulation) in the European Union looms like a Colossus. It dictates stringent rules for data handling that can make even seasoned data handlers sweat under their collars. Failing to comply isn't just a slap on the wrist—it can result in fines hefty enough to make a pirate's treasure trove look like pocket change. Imagine trying to conduct your orchestra (your business) when the GDPR is the strict conductor, tapping his baton impatiently.

Across the pond, you encounter the CCPA (California Consumer Privacy Act) and other U.S. state-specific legislations, each with its own set of rules and penalties, making the task of compliance feel like trying to juggle flaming torches while reciting the Declaration of Independence. It's a thrilling act that requires precision, focus, and a lot of practice.

Moreover, when you step into the realm of specific industries like healthcare or finance, additional layers of

regulatory intricacies unfold. HIPAA (Health Insurance Portability and Accountability Act) in healthcare, for example, demands rigorous safeguards for patient data, treating it with more reverence than ancient sacred texts. Or consider the financial sector regulated by the likes of FINRA or the SEC, where AI's role in predictive analytics and customer interactions must be transparent as crystal and firm as diamond.

How then does one not only comply with these multifarious regulations but also use them as a stepladder to success? Here's a guide carved out of the dense regulatory thicket:

Develop a robust regulatory compliance framework tailored to your specific industry and the jurisdictions you operate within. Think of it as crafting a map that highlights safe passages through pirate-infested waters.

Stay abreast of legislative changes and updates. It's like being a weather forecaster for regulatory climates—always prepared, never surprised. Employ legal experts or use regulatory technology services that keep you updated in real-time.

Can Artificial Intelligence Really Help Me Make Money? Here Is How

Implement rigorous data governance practices. Treat data like the crown jewels: heavily guarded, meticulously tracked, and only shared with the utmost discretion and security.

Educate your team regularly on compliance matters. Turn these training sessions into engaging workshops rather than drudgery-filled lectures—think less high school detention, more captivating TED Talk.

Engage proactively with regulators. Don't wait for them to come knocking with a fine in hand. Be proactive, seek advice, and even participate in shaping the dialogue around AI regulation in your sector.

By mastering these strategies, not only do you shield your business from the potential pitfalls of non-compliance, but you also forge a reputation as a trustworthy, reliable player in the AI arena. This isn't just about avoiding penalties—it's about building a brand that stands for integrity and innovation, ensuring that your AI-powered ventures are as above board as they are profitable. In the grand casino of AI business strategies, consider compliance not as a begrudged minimum bet but as a savvy investment in your company's reputation and operational longevity. After all, in

the high-stakes game of AI entrepreneurship, it's better to play by the rules than to be played by them.

Chapter 7: Success Stories of AI Millionaires

In the bustling bazaar of modern commerce, where entrepreneurs and visionaries hustle like medieval merchants, a few daring souls have not just entered the market but have danced through it with AI as their partner, turning data streams into rivers of gold. These are the mavericks who've ridden the wild AI stallion to the lush valleys of success, proving that when wielded wisely, AI is not just a tool but a treasure trove.

Imagine the first of our champions, an audacious entrepreneur who, armed with algorithms more intricate than a spider's web, revolutionized the retail industry. They deployed AI to predict consumer purchasing patterns with the precision of an oracle. This wasn't just about guessing which color of socks would sell better next season; it was a deep, neural-network-driven analysis that anticipated trends before they emerged, stocked shelves virtually, and personalized marketing to a degree that made consumers feel as if the ads were reading their minds. The result? A

dramatic uptick in sales, customer satisfaction soaring sky-high, and a business that scaled globally faster than one could say "artificial intelligence."

Then there's the wizard of the financial sector, who employed AI not merely as a calculator but as a crystal ball. This fintech savant used machine learning to navigate the volatile seas of stock trading, with AI algorithms that detected subtle market shifts, analyzing vast amounts of financial data to make predictions with uncanny accuracy. Their platform became indispensable to traders around the globe, turning a modest startup into a behemoth that outshone traditional financial institutions, making our protagonist not just a millionaire but a disruptor of Wall Street itself.

But let's not forget the healthcare hero who harnessed AI to personalize medicine in ways that were once the stuff of science fiction. By integrating AI with genomic data, this pioneer created a platform that suggested custom treatment plans for patients with chronic illnesses, drastically improving outcomes. The AI sifted through medical records and genetic information to recommend perfectly tailored therapies, turning a once-cumbersome process into a

streamlined dance of data and decision-making. The impact? A healthcare revolution and a personal fortune built on the grateful smiles of millions of patients.

And in the realm of marketing, consider the digital artist who turned data into dollars. This visionary used AI-driven analytics to craft marketing campaigns with surgical precision, targeting consumers based on behavior, preferences, and even mood. Their campaigns were so effective, so eerily accurate in their appeal, that consumer engagement rates exploded, catapulting a humble digital marketing firm into the stratosphere of industry leaders.

Leverage AI for predictive analytics in whatever niche you dominate, be it retail, finance, healthcare, or any sector ripe for disruption.

Invest in machine learning platforms that can sift through and make sense of big data, providing insights not readily apparent to human analysts.

Adopt AI-driven personalization techniques to tailor your products or services to individual customer needs, enhancing satisfaction and loyalty.

Utilize AI for real-time decision-making, allowing you to respond to market changes swiftly and strategically.

Can Artificial Intelligence Really Help Me Make Money? Here Is How

Ensure your AI solutions are scalable, ready to grow with your business as you expand from local markets to global territories.

By emulating these pioneers, not only might you find yourself a fortune in your chosen field, but you could also join the ranks of those rare visionaries who've reshaped industries and redefined what's possible. So, strap on your entrepreneurial jetpack, powered by AI, and prepare to blast off into a future where your name might just be synonymous with innovation and success. Remember, in the gold rush of AI, it's not just about finding nuggets on the ground—it's about using the right tools to mine, refine, and, most importantly, shine.

In the mesmerizing theatre of modern commerce, where innovation is the ticket to entry and disruption the standing ovation, AI has ushered in not merely a new act but an entirely new genre of business models. These paradigms, infused with the intelligence of machines, are not just rewriting the rules of the game; they are designing a whole new gameboard.

Picture a startup that, instead of selling products, offers AI-driven insights as a service, transforming raw,

unstructured data into a polished, predictive power tool for any business, from bakeries to brokerage firms. This isn't just about offering analytics; it's about providing a sixth sense for market dynamics. Here, AI algorithms analyze everything from consumer behavior to macroeconomic indicators, delivering bespoke insights that businesses can subscribe to, like a magazine, but instead of fashion and gossip, they get foresight and facts.

Then, imagine a company that has turned AI into an art form, literally. This enterprise uses neural networks to create unique artworks, blending millions of colors and styles from classic and contemporary art to produce pieces so unique they could hang in the Louvre (or at least in the digital equivalent). Here, patrons don't just buy a painting; they commission an AI to create a visual expression that's never been seen before, making every purchase a personal revolution in artistry.

Consider also the world of autonomous finance, where an AI firm provides not just advice but active management of your investments. Like a financial concierge with an algorithmic brain, this AI doesn't just suggest where to invest but actually makes the investments, monitors them, and

optimizes the portfolio in real-time based on shifting market sands. It's as if you had a Wall Street veteran sleeping on your couch, constantly mumbling stock tips in their sleep, except it's all happening in the cloud.

And what about a venture that leverages AI for environmental good? This company uses satellite imagery and AI to monitor deforestation, coral bleaching, or urban expansion in real-time, providing invaluable data to governments, NGOs, and even tourists who want to visit sites without contributing to their degradation. It's like having an omnipresent guardian angel who not only watches over Earth's natural treasures but also arms its protectors with the information needed to defend it.

For those ready to dive into the AI revolution and carve out their own niche in this lucrative arena:

Develop a scalable AI platform that can be tailored to specific industries or needs, allowing you to offer personalization at scale.

Leverage AI to tap into new forms of creativity, whether in art, music, or design, creating products that stand out in a crowded market.

Can Artificial Intelligence Really Help Me Make Money? Here Is How

Use AI to provide dynamic pricing models for your services, adjusting in real-time based on demand, competition, and customer behavior.

Explore AI applications in non-traditional areas like environmental monitoring or urban planning, where technology meets social good.

Keep your AI models transparent and ethical, ensuring that your business not only leads in innovation but also in integrity.

Embrace these AI-driven business models with the zeal of a Silicon Valley disruptor and the precision of a Swiss watchmaker. The result? A business that not only profits but also propels the world forward, proving that the best way to predict the future is to invent it. And who knows? With a bit of ingenuity and a lot of data, the next AI millionaire could indeed be you.

Embarking on the journey from a mere concept etched on a napkin to a thriving business with AI at its core is akin to navigating a thrilling rollercoaster designed by a mad scientist — exhilarating highs, terrifying drops, and loops that twist your perspective until you're not sure which way is up. It's a ride not for the faint of heart, yet for those daring

souls who strap in, the potential rewards can catapult you into the stratosphere of success.

Imagine the humble beginnings, where our intrepid entrepreneur — let's call her Ada — starts with nothing but a brilliant idea and a gritty determination to change the world. The first stage, the conception, is all about brewing the perfect storm of innovation. Ada spends nights hunched over her laptop, coding furiously, fueled by the potent combination of caffeine and dreams. She's not just creating software; she's architecting a future.

As dawn breaks on her fledgling startup, Ada enters the seed stage, where her focus shifts to planting her digital seeds into fertile ground. This involves crafting a minimum viable product (MVP), a prototype that embodies her vision yet is functional enough to entice early adopters. It's her first taste of turning the theoretical into the tangible, a digital alchemist turning code into gold.

Now comes the nurturing phase. Ada's MVP is out in the wild, and feedback flows in like a cascade of data. Every user interaction, every bug report is a nugget of wisdom that Ada uses to refine her creation. This stage is iterative, a loop of launch, learn, and refine, which Ada navigates with

the agility of a cat on a hot tin roof. The startup is more than a business now; it's a living organism, evolving with each cycle.

Growth is where the magic happens. Ada's startup begins to scale, propelled by the dual engines of increasing user adoption and burgeoning investor interest. Here, AI isn't just a tool; it's a catalyst, enhancing every aspect of the business, from optimizing user experience to automating back-end processes. Sales soar, the user base grows, and Ada finds herself not at the end, but at a thrilling new beginning.

Yet, success is not a summit but a plateau, a new vantage point from which Ada can see further, dream bigger. The expansion phase sees her startup branching out, exploring new markets, integrating additional AI capabilities, perhaps even leveraging machine learning to breach into new industries. It's an empire in the making, and AI is her general, strategizing each move with precision.

Start with a solid MVP that not only addresses a genuine need but does so with enough flair to capture attention and imagination.

Can Artificial Intelligence Really Help Me Make Money? Here Is How

Engage with your user base; their feedback is the compass that will guide your iterations and improvements. Treat every critique as a gift, each praise as a map to your next destination.

Secure funding not just with promises, but with proof. Show potential investors a trajectory of growth, a narrative of potential fueled by real data.

Use AI not just as a backend tool but as a front of shop excellence. Let it enhance the customer experience, streamline operations, and uncover new opportunities.

Scale wisely, ensuring that each step forward is sustainable. Adopt new technologies, expand into new markets, but always with one eye on the foundation, ensuring it's strong enough to support your expanded vision.

Ada's journey from startup to success is more than a tale of making money; it's a blueprint for revolutionizing industries, changing lives, and challenging the status quo. And as you chart your own course through the tumult of entrepreneurship, remember, each challenge is but a stepping stone to greater heights, each failure a lesson to be learned. With AI as your ally and innovation as your compass, the sky's not the limit—it's just another milestone.

Can Artificial Intelligence Really Help Me Make Money? Here Is How

Embarking on a venture in the wild world of AI is akin to setting sail on the high seas with a map that promises treasure. Some intrepid explorers strike gold, while others find themselves adrift, perhaps sinking under the weight of their own ambitions. The tales of those who didn't find their X on the first try are not just cautionary—they are treasure maps in themselves, marked with 'Here Be Dragons' warnings that guide future adventurers away from treacherous waters.

Picture the eager entrepreneur, let's call him Archibald, who launched an AI-driven startup with dreams as high as the Ritz. Archibald's venture, which aimed to automate gourmet cooking through a robotic chef, sizzled with potential. Yet, his dream soufflé fell flat due to a critical oversight: he hadn't considered the complexity of taste preferences and the artistry involved in haute cuisine. The lesson? AI can crunch data and follow recipes, but it can't taste test a sauce or savor the aroma of truffle oil. It was a stark reminder that AI, for all its prowess, lacks the subtleties of human senses which are often crucial in industries that cater to them.

Then there was Beatrice, the whiz-kid coder who developed an AI system for legal firms, designed to sift through case files and predict trial outcomes. A sterling idea on paper, but in practice, it buckled under the sheer variability of human behavior and legal nuances. Her AI couldn't capture the jury's emotions or the persuasive power of a seasoned attorney. Beatrice's tale underscored that AI struggles in arenas where emotional intelligence and human interaction play pivotal roles.

And who could forget the story of Cornelius, whose AI startup aimed at revolutionizing education by personalizing learning at scale? His vision was grand—AI tutors for every student, providing tailored lessons and feedback. However, Cornelius underestimated the immense diversity of learning styles, the need for human empathy in teaching, and the regulatory mazes surrounding educational data. His endeavor taught us that while AI can offer significant support in education, the human touch remains irreplaceable, and privacy concerns are paramount.

From these misadventures, a repository of rich, invaluable lessons emerges:

Can Artificial Intelligence Really Help Me Make Money? Here Is How

Understand AI's limitations. Appreciate where AI can excel and where it may falter, especially in fields requiring deep emotional intelligence, creativity, or sensory inputs.

Engage with your target audience early and often. Validate your assumptions and ensure that there is a genuine demand for your AI-driven solution. Continuous feedback is crucial for steering the project in the right direction.

Compliance and privacy must be at the forefront. Especially in sectors like healthcare and education, understanding and integrating these considerations from the get-go is essential.

Pilot extensively before full-scale implementation. Test your AI solution in controlled environments and be ready to pivot based on what the data tells you.

Foster an adaptive business plan. Remain flexible and responsive to technology and market changes. AI evolves rapidly; your business strategy should keep pace.

Embarking on an AI enterprise, successful or otherwise, is not for the meek. It requires the audacity of a pirate and the wisdom of a sage. The failures of past ventures aren't just mishaps; they are beacons that light the way for future

success. So, if you're gearing up to launch your own AI-driven ship, chart a course informed by these tales of yore. With AI as your compass and lessons learned as your guide, who knows? The next chapter of success in this high-tech saga could very well bear your name.

In the electrifying theater of AI startups, where ambition meets innovation at the crossroads of future tech, venture capital plays the role of the grand impresario, ushering in the next act with the flourish of capital infusion. Think of venture capitalists (VCs) not just as stodgy financiers in bespoke suits but as modern-day Midases, whose touch can turn nascent ideas into golden enterprises bustling with potential.

Imagine a realm where every fledgling startup is a sprouting beanstalk reaching for the sky, and venture capital is the rain that nourishes them, allowing them to grow, twist, and climb towards the clouds of market success. However, this rain doesn't just fall from the sky; it's a calculated deluge directed towards plots of land—startups—that promise the most fertile outcomes. These VCs scour the landscape with an eagle's eye, looking for the greenest shoots, the most robust seedlings in the tech forest—those employing AI in ways that disrupt, enhance, and innovate.

But here's the kicker: securing venture capital isn't just about having a groundbreaking idea or a killer product; it's about storytelling. Yes, you heard that right—every successful pitch is a saga, woven with threads of potential profits, market disruption, and strategic execution. The protagonist (that's you) must convince these modern-day patrons of commerce that your AI venture is the next big plot twist in the narrative of technological evolution.

Think of your venture as a ship setting off on a treasure hunt. In this narrative, venture capitalists are less interested in the ship itself and more in the map you possess—the business plan. They want to see Xs marking spots not just of buried treasure, but of new territories—markets yet to be explored and conquered. They seek a crew (your team) who can navigate turbulent waters, a captain (you again) who can lead through storms; they are investing in the journey, the adventure, and the promise of treasure, all made more attainable through the prowess of AI.

Once the investment is secured, the role of venture capital shifts from patron to co-navigator. They're not just silent sponsors; they're active participants in charting the course. With resources beyond mere money—networks,

industry insights, managerial expertise—VCs help steer the startup through scaling seas, from beta versions to major market launches, from initial traction to widespread adoption.

For those daring to draw venture capital to their AI odyssey, here are some strategies straight from the captain's log:

Craft a compelling narrative around your AI solution. How will it change the landscape, disrupt the market, or address a burning need? Be specific, be passionate, and above all, be clear.

Demonstrate scalability and potential for return on investment. Venture capitalists are treasure hunters at heart; they need to see the map leading to gold, which in business terms translates to profit margins and market reach.

Showcase your team's expertise and commitment. Investors bet on jockeys as much as they do on horses. Ensure your team has the skills, drive, and resilience to see the journey through.

Be prepared with data to back up your claims. Whether it's market research, early testing results, or theoretical

models, bring proof to the table that your AI isn't just smoke and mirrors but a veritable engine of potential growth.

Understand the landscape of AI regulation and innovation. Be informed about how shifts in policy or technology could impact your business, and be ready to discuss how you'll navigate these changes.

Navigating the world of venture capital as an AI startup is like weaving through a regatta where every ship is as swift and sleek as yours. With the right preparation, a clear course, and a bit of that old sea-dog charm, you can catch the wind, attract the VCs, and sail towards that horizon where success—and maybe a chest or two of gold—awaits. So hoist the sails, plot your course, and may the venture winds be ever in your favor!

Please Leave a Review

Did this book tickle your techy taste buds and boost your money-making brainpower? If you had a blast flipping through these chapters and found the golden nuggets of financial wisdom you were after, I have a tiny favor to ask.

Imagine the joy of countless readers, just like you, discovering this gem thanks to your rave review. You'll be a hero, a guiding star in their quest for AI money-making enlightenment! Plus, think of all the good karma points you'll rack up (the financial type, of course).

So, if you're feeling the love, click this review link (or point your phone camera to this QR code) and let the world know how this book rocked your world (and bank account). I (and future readers) will thank you from the bottom of our silicon hearts!

Click Here to Leave Review

Chapter 8: Integrating AI into Other Technologies

In the magical digital era, where the melding of technologies creates landscapes more varied and vibrant than a techno-futurist's wildest dreams, the marriage of AI and blockchain emerges as a powerhouse duo. Imagine AI as the brilliant but somewhat scatterbrained professor, bursting with ideas but occasionally forgetful about locking the lab door. Enter blockchain, the meticulous, methodical librarian, keeping every book—nay, every byte—in impeccable order and under lock and key. Together, they form a partnership that is as secure as it is cerebral, turning your venture into a veritable Fort Knox of data integrity and innovation.

First, let's dive into the mechanics of this formidable alliance. AI is all about learning patterns, making decisions, and automating complex processes with speed and efficiency that mimic—and often surpass—the human brain. However, these systems can be as vulnerable as they are powerful, open to attacks from data breaches to algorithmic

biases. Here, blockchain steps in like an unbreachable digital fortress. With its decentralized structure and cryptographic security measures, blockchain ensures that each piece of data processed by AI is recorded, immutable, and transparent. It's like every piece of data gets its own unalterable diary entry, witnessed by a crowd that can't be bribed or manipulated.

Consider a practical application in the realm of financial services, where AI-driven algorithms assess loan eligibility or manage investments. By integrating blockchain, every decision, every transaction is recorded on a transparent, tamper-proof ledger. No more dark corners where discrepancies can lurk; everything is illuminated under the clear, hard light of blockchain's scrutiny. It's not just about preventing fraud; it's about building a foundation of trust that's rock-solid.

Or, look to the supply chain, where AI can predict shortages and optimize routes, but the addition of blockchain provides an indelible record of every product's journey. This integration not only enhances efficiency but also ensures compliance and authenticity, which in today's global market, is as valuable as the goods being shipped.

Imagine a world where counterfeit goods are as outdated as dial-up internet, all thanks to the vigilant watch of AI and blockchain combined.

Now, for those venturing into this hybrid technology landscape, the path is strewn with golden opportunities but requires careful navigation. Here's how you might proceed:

Understand the strengths and limitations of both technologies. AI is your go-to for processing vast amounts of data and learning from it, while blockchain is your stalwart guardian, ensuring that every learning, every data point, is secure and verifiable.

Identify use cases where the combination adds value. Not every application needs the Fort Knox treatment. Focus on areas where security, transparency, and data integrity are paramount.

Develop skills or partnerships specializing in both AI and blockchain. The intersection of these technologies is a niche but growing field, offering rich rewards for those who master it.

Prioritize transparency and user trust. Use this technology pairing to not just secure data, but also to shine

a light on your processes, winning customer trust through unparalleled accountability.

Keep abreast of regulatory changes. As both AI and blockchain reshape industries, they also attract regulatory attention. Staying informed and compliant is not just good practice; it's a survival strategy.

Integrating AI with blockchain is not merely adding a layer of security; it's about reimagining what's possible at the intersection of data intelligence and incorruptible record-keeping. For the savvy entrepreneur, this combination isn't just a strategy; it's a revolution—one that promises not just to protect your venture, but to propel it into a new realm of credibility and success. So, as you chart your course through these technologically tumultuous waters, consider this duo your twin engines, powering you towards a horizon glittering with potential.

In the fantastical world where technology melds and meshes in an intricate dance of data and devices, the coupling of Artificial Intelligence with the Internet of Things (IoT) emerges as the ultimate pas de deux. This dynamic duo, when harmonized, is not just additive; it's multiplicative, creating a synergy that propels mundane objects into the

realm of smart technology and transforms raw data into actionable intelligence. Imagine a scenario where your toaster chats amiably with your alarm clock to ensure your bread pops up the moment you shuffle bleary-eyed into the kitchen. That's just breakfast, now imagine that kind of coordination in an industrial scale!

AI serves as the brain, interpreting and learning from the data, while IoT acts as the limbs, executing actions in the physical world based on AI's decisions. Together, they perform a ballet of functionality that can turn a simple home into a smart home, a conventional factory into a smart factory, and mundane objects into interconnected, interactive smart devices capable of optimizing themselves without human intervention.

Picture this: IoT devices spread across a factory floor, collecting data on everything from machine efficiency to energy usage. Alone, they provide a data stream; with AI, they provide insights. AI analyses this flood of information in real time, identifying patterns, predicting when a machine is likely to fail or when energy consumption will peak. Armed with this foresight, AI can preemptively adjust workflows, shut down unnecessary systems, or alert human operators,

thus preventing downtime, saving energy, and reducing costs—turning what is traditionally seen as clairvoyance into a standard operational procedure.

In the realm of healthcare, the amalgamation of AI and IoT takes a particularly exhilarating turn. Consider wearable devices that monitor everything from heart rates to glucose levels. These devices collect vital data continuously, but without AI, this data might just remain a series of numbers. AI transforms these numbers into health insights, sending alerts for anomalies that could indicate a need for medical intervention, scheduling doctor appointments, or even triggering emergency responses. It's like having a doctor in your pocket, watching over you with the vigilance of a hawk without the need to perch in a waiting room.

And let's not overlook the urban landscapes, where smart cities harness the power of AI and IoT to manage everything from traffic to pollution. Here, sensors collect data on traffic flow, air quality, and public safety, while AI analyzes this data to optimize traffic lights, divert vehicles from congested areas, and notify authorities of potential hazards. It's as if the city itself comes alive, breathing in

data and exhaling operational excellence, creating an environment as responsive as it is efficient.

For those intrepid souls eager to harness this powerhouse combination in their own entrepreneurial quests, here's how to embark:

Identify areas within your business where data collection overlaps with operational execution. These are your hotspots for AI and IoT integration.

Invest in IoT infrastructure that communicates seamlessly. Ensure that your devices can talk to each other and to a central AI system without getting lost in translation.

Develop or integrate AI systems that can not only analyze data but also learn from it. You want a system that gets smarter over time, fine-tuning its algorithms to your specific operational rhythms.

Focus on scalability and security. As your network of IoT devices grows, ensure your AI can scale accordingly, and that data remains secure from external threats—a fortress as much as a brain.

Stay abreast of advances in both AI and IoT. The landscape is evolving rapidly; keeping your knowledge base updated is as crucial as updating your software.

Can Artificial Intelligence Really Help Me Make Money? Here Is How

By weaving AI with IoT into the fabric of your business operations, you create not just a network of devices but a mesh of intelligence, capable of elevating your business to levels of efficiency and insight previously relegated to the realm of science fiction. So, gear up, for when AI meets IoT, the possibilities are not just exciting—they're exponential.

In the grand cosmic parade of technological marvels, where Artificial Intelligence dances in lockstep with its digital brethren, the pairing with Augmented Reality (AR) emerges as a spectacle of unprecedented wonder. This duo, akin to an alchemist's dream, transforms the mundane into the magical, merging the digital and physical realms into an interactive tapestry that not only enchants but also enhances business capabilities in ways that stir the pot of profitability with a silver-laden ladle.

Imagine the bustling marketplace of retail, where AR brings products to life right before the customer's eyes, and AI whispers in the background, analyzing behaviors, preferences, and purchasing patterns. Together, they create a shopping experience that is as personalized as it is mesmerizing. Customers no longer just browse products; they interact with them, viewing digital overlays that show

how that sofa might look in their living room or how that jacket might fit. It's like having a fairy godmother, but instead of turning pumpkins into carriages, she turns browsing into buying.

Step into the world of training and education, where this blend of AI and AR doesn't just inform; it immerses. Trainees in industries from surgery to plumbing can practice their skills in a simulated, augmented environment where every action is monitored, analyzed, and enhanced by AI. Mistakes are not just corrected; they're understood and learned from, providing a feedback loop that is as rich as it is rapid. It's like training with a wise old mentor who not only watches your every move but also provides instant, invaluable feedback.

Consider also the realm of marketing and advertising, where the fusion of AI and AR creates campaigns that capture not just the eyes but the imagination. Billboards transform into interactive experiences, and product demos leap off the page—literally. With AI's data-driven insights ensuring that these augmented experiences reach the right people at the right time, engagement rates soar as high as

an eagle on an updraft, and conversion rates follow suit, climbing the proverbial ladder to revenue heaven.

In customer service, the integration of AI and AR turns mundane interactions into dynamic solutions. Imagine a customer struggling to assemble a piece of furniture — a common battlefield for many. With AR, they can point their phone's camera at the troublesome furniture piece, and AI overlays step-by-step, augmented instructions, turning frustration into accomplishment. It's customer support that feels like having a wise guide right there in the room, turning screws and fitting pieces alongside you.

For the trailblazing entrepreneur keen to harness this formidable alliance:

Develop AR applications that allow customers to visualize your products in their own space, leveraging AI to personalize and enhance these visualizations based on user data and preferences.

Incorporate AR into your training protocols, using AI to adapt scenarios and difficulty levels in real-time based on the trainee's progress and performance.

Can Artificial Intelligence Really Help Me Make Money? Here Is How

Utilize AI-driven AR in marketing to create interactive adverts that not only catch the eye but also engage the user, providing personalized content that shifts dynamically according to the data captured on user interactions.

Explore AR customer service tools, enhanced by AI to provide not just automated responses but context-aware solutions, reducing response times and increasing customer satisfaction.

By merging AI with AR, businesses can not only step into a new frontier of digital interaction but also forge a path where every customer interaction is an opportunity, every training session is a revelation, and every marketing campaign is a spectacle. This isn't just riding the wave of technological innovation; it's making the wave, guiding it, and watching as it reshapes the landscape of your industry. So, gear up, for the future isn't just coming; it's already here, and it's augmented.

In the magical circus of technological advancements, where AI juggles data and algorithms with the finesse of a seasoned performer, the emergence of quantum computing is akin to adding a quantum trapeze to the act—swinging higher, faster, and with more dazzling complexity than ever

before. This isn't just another incremental step in computing; it's a quantum leap into a realm where the rules of physics operate on a bafflingly minuscule scale, yet their implications are as gargantuan as the potential profits.

Quantum computing, with its ability to handle vast datasets and perform calculations at speeds unfathomable to traditional binary systems, propels AI from a tool of iterative learning to a titan of immediate insight. Imagine a scenario where an AI system, powered by quantum computing, can simulate and predict complex chemical reactions for drug discovery in moments, a task that would take classical computers years. This isn't just speeding up the process; it's like turning a horse-drawn carriage into a hyperloop.

The impact on AI's problem-solving capabilities is equally groundbreaking. Quantum computers can analyze and optimize large systems almost instantaneously—from climate models and traffic systems to financial markets and logistics networks—providing AI with the ability to not just react to the world, but to reimagine it. It's as if AI has been given a crystal ball, except this one doesn't predict the future; it helps create it.

Can Artificial Intelligence Really Help Me Make Money? Here Is How

For industries banking on AI to parse through complex patterns and predictions, such as in AI-driven hedge funds or predictive maintenance for manufacturing, the integration of quantum computing converts what were once educated guesses into near-certain foresights. The implications are profound, stretching the fabric of current capabilities into a tapestry of possibilities that covers new markets and opportunities. It's like playing chess with a supercomputer against opponents still strategizing on checkerboards.

Yet, the road to quantum AI is sprinkled with both stardust and stumbling blocks. The sheer power of quantum computing brings with it not just complexities in technology and implementation but also in security. Quantum computers could one day crack codes that protect our most sensitive data, meaning that AI systems must evolve not just in capability, but also in cybersecurity measures. It's a technological arms race, where the shields must evolve as quickly as the swords.

Invest time in familiarizing with quantum-ready AI research and development. The future belongs to those who prepare for it today. By understanding quantum algorithms

and their applications in AI, you can position your business at the frontier of this new wave.

Collaborate with quantum technology pioneers. Whether through partnerships with academia, industry, or specialized startups, collaboration can provide you with a quantum leap in expertise and technology.

Educate your team about the potentials and challenges of quantum AI. As the quantum future approaches, a well-informed team is your best asset.

Develop a quantum cybersecurity strategy. With great power comes great responsibility; ensure that your quantum AI implementations are secure from both current and future threats.

Stay agile and informed. The field of quantum computing is evolving at a breathtaking pace. Keeping abreast of the latest developments and being ready to pivot your strategies accordingly is crucial.

By integrating AI with quantum computing, businesses are not just adopting a new technology; they are stepping into a new era of possibilities. This union promises to redefine industries, turning the unimaginable into the achievable. As quantum computing continues to develop, it

will not just support AI; it will expand its horizons, enhancing its ability to think, analyze, and interact with the world in ways we can scarcely imagine. Thus, in the grand cosmic ballet of tech, quantum computing and AI together perform a dance that could one day choreograph the future of humanity itself.

Imagine a future where the fusion of AI and robotics creates not merely machines, but symphonies of mechanical precision and intellectual prowess, a dazzling duet where silicon brains and steel bodies dance to the rhythm of innovation and efficiency. In this near-magical realm, robotics don't just perform tasks; they anticipate needs, adapt to challenges, and evolve from mere tools to partners in progress. AI serves as the maestro, conducting these robotic orchestras with algorithms that can predict, learn, and optimize in real-time. This isn't the stuff of sci-fi fantasies; it's the blueprint for a revolution in how business, technology, and daily human activities intertwine.

Consider the impact on manufacturing where AI-driven robots can not only assemble parts with inhuman speed and precision but also foresee mechanical failures and maintenance needs, perhaps even ordering parts and

scheduling repairs without human intervention. It's like having an auto-mechanic who's always on duty, with an oil can in one hand and a wrench in the other, ensuring everything runs smoothly. The result? Downtime plummets, productivity soars, and human workers can focus on creative and strategic tasks beyond the reach of robotic capabilities.

Then there's the realm of healthcare, where robotic surgery, guided by AI's unblinking eye, achieves new heights of precision. Surgical robots, controlled by AI, can perform complex procedures with minimal incisions, guided by real-time data that no human surgeon could process at the same speed. Imagine a robotic arm that's as steady as a rock but as delicate as a brushstroke, powered by AI that's consumed every piece of relevant medical research ever recorded. Patients recover faster, hospitals stay efficient, and surgeons become superheroes with robotic sidekicks.

In retail, AI-enhanced robots transform inventory management into a high-speed ballet of efficiency. These robots scan shelves, track products, and even restock items based on predictive analytics that anticipate customer buying patterns. It's as if each robot is a personal shopper,

not just for the customers but for the store itself, maintaining an optimal flow of goods to shelves just as shoppers need them.

But the plot thickens when we add autonomous vehicles into the mix. AI and robotics blend to navigate roads with a precision and safety record that outstrips even the most attentive human driver. Delivery trucks, taxis, and even public transport become safer, more efficient, and less dependent on human reflexes. It's like each vehicle is piloted by a chauffeur with superhuman reflexes and an infallible sense of direction, only without the need for coffee breaks or sleep.

For the daring entrepreneur, here are several forward-thinking strategies to capitalize on this confluence of AI and robotics:

Invest time in familiarizing in robotics startups that are spearheading innovations in industries relevant to your interests. Whether it's healthcare, manufacturing, or logistics, being an early adopter can position you at the forefront of the market.

Develop partnerships with tech developers to create custom solutions for your business needs. Tailored robotics

powered by cutting-edge AI can provide you with a competitive edge that's difficult to replicate.

Focus on upskilling your workforce to work alongside these advanced robots, ensuring that human employees can maximize the benefits of robotic coworkers by focusing on oversight, maintenance, and enhancement of robotic tasks.

Implement scalable solutions that can grow with your business. Start small with a single robotic application, then expand as you refine your approach and learn what works best in your specific context.

Stay informed about regulatory changes and ethical considerations in AI and robotics to ensure your business remains compliant and socially responsible as these technologies evolve.

By embracing the dynamic duo of AI and robotics, you're not just preparing for the future; you're actively shaping it, crafting a world where technology doesn't just support the human experience but enhances it, making every task more efficient, every job safer, and every industry more innovative. So strap in, power up, and let AI and robotics propel your entrepreneurial journey into this brave new era of limitless potential.

Chapter 9: From Concept to Cash: Practical AI Applications

In the bustling bazaar of modern industry, where every booth and stall brims with innovations, AI is the charismatic shopkeeper who knows just what you need before you even ask. From automating mundane tasks to solving complex problems that baffle human minds, AI's tentacles stretch across various sectors, transforming theoretical potentials into hefty profits with a flair that would make even the most stoic investor crack a smile.

Dive into the world of agriculture, where AI is not just a tool but a revolution in green boots. Here, AI-driven drones hover over vast fields, their cameras scrutinizing crops with the keen eyes of an eagle. These high-flying sentinels assess plant health, predict yields, and even detect early signs of disease or pestilence. Below, AI-powered tractors navigate rows with precision, deploying water and pesticides with an efficiency that conserves resources while maximizing output. It's as if the scarecrow from Oz got a

degree in agronomy and took to the skies, ensuring that no leaf goes unturned and every grain of potential is harvested.

Transition to the realm of finance, where AI acts as both sentinel and sage. Algorithms analyze market data with a voracity that would exhaust any human counterpart, predicting fluctuations with a precision that borders on prescience. Automated trading systems make split-second decisions, executing trades at volumes and speeds that boggle the mind. Meanwhile, AI in fintech innovates in risk assessment, customizing loan offers based on a dizzying array of factors, from spending patterns to social media behavior. It's like having a financial wizard for a friend, one who's equally at home predicting stock rises as they are sifting through your spending habits to advise on budgeting.

Step into the world of healthcare, where AI dons a white coat and wields data like a scalpel. In diagnostics, machine learning algorithms digest medical imaging data, spotting anomalies with a precision that human eyes might miss. On the treatment front, AI systems analyze patient data to suggest customized treatment plans that account for everything from genetic factors to lifestyle. It's as if Dr. House had a love child with a supercomputer, diagnosing

diseases with a deductive prowess that's untainted by sarcasm.

In the sphere of customer service, AI morphs into a chameleon, blending seamlessly into interactions via chatbots and virtual assistants. These AI entities provide 24/7 customer support, handling inquiries, complaints, and even making sales recommendations with a politeness that never wanes. They learn from each interaction, continuously improving their responses and strategies to enhance customer satisfaction. It's as though the genie from Aladdin got a job after the wishes were done, charming customers around the clock without ever needing to go back into the lamp.

In agriculture, invest in AI technologies that enhance yield prediction and resource management. Start small with pilot areas, scale up as AI proves its worth in green returns.

In finance, integrate AI to enhance decision-making processes. Ensure robust security measures to foster trust and safeguard against potential AI vulnerabilities.

Leverage AI in healthcare for predictive diagnostics and personalized treatment plans. Collaborate with medical

professionals to ensure the AI tools complement and enhance rather than overshadow human expertise.

Utilize AI-driven chatbots in customer service to enhance user engagement and operational efficiency. Constantly update conversational models to maintain relevance and effectiveness.

By harnessing AI's capabilities across these diverse landscapes, businesses can transform everyday operations into extraordinary profits, proving that in the modern marketplace, AI is not just a tool but a transformative force, reshaping industries from the ground up. So gear up, plot your course, and let AI navigate your entrepreneurial ship across these lucrative waters.

In the teeming digital marketplace where e-commerce reigns supreme, AI has donned the cap of a personal shopping assistant with the knack of a seasoned market vendor who knows not just what you want to buy but what you might fancy even before you fancy it. This isn't merely a trick or a gimmick but a profound transformation of shopping into a highly personalized experience, powered by

algorithms that can predict desires with an accuracy that might seem, at times, downright spooky.

Picture this: a shopper, let's call her Ella, enters an online store. The moment she lands on the page, AI kicks into high gear. It isn't her first visit, and the AI knows her browsing habits better than she might know herself. It quickly scans its trove of data—past purchases, viewed items, lingered-over products—and within milliseconds, the webpage Ella sees is subtly transformed. It's as if the digital shelves rearrange themselves before her very eyes, presenting her with items that tickle her fancy, nudge at her desires, or gently whisper to her needs.

This AI doesn't stop at mere suggestions. It analyzes Ella's dwell time on product pages, her zooms on images, her hovers over descriptions. Each interaction feeds into a dynamic learning loop, refining the AI's understanding of her preferences. The AI tailors email campaigns specifically for Ella, featuring items left in her cart, suggesting similar products, or alerting her to flash sales on her favorite brands. It's like having a personal shopper who's always thinking about what you might need next, bringing it to you with a digital smile.

Moreover, the AI's capabilities extend to managing inventory by predicting trends and adjusting stock levels based on real-time sales data and forecasted demands. It's as if the backend of the store operates with a crystal ball, ensuring popular items never run out and less popular ones don't languish on virtual shelves. This level of operational efficiency not only boosts sales but also enhances customer satisfaction because what Ella wants is always in stock.

And let's not forget the power of AI-driven analytics. This tool doesn't just personalize; it provides a bird's-eye view of customer journeys, pinpointing where potential buyers drop off and why. It identifies patterns that might suggest why a particular product isn't selling, or why another unexpectedly flies off the virtual shelves. It's like having a detective on the case, one who's good with numbers and keen on customer moods.

Implement AI-driven recommendation engines to personalize user experiences dynamically. Make every visitor feel like the store was designed just for them.

Use AI to craft personalized marketing messages. Send emails that address the customer by name, refer to their preferences, and offer relevant deals.

Deploy AI for predictive analytics in inventory management. Keep your best sellers in stock and identify new opportunities based on emerging trends.

Optimize price dynamically using AI algorithms that consider demand, competitor pricing, and price sensitivity to maximize profits while remaining competitive.

Continuously refine your AI models based on customer feedback and interaction data. The market evolves, and so should your AI, adapting to shifts in consumer behavior and preferences.

In the e-commerce arena, AI becomes not just a tool but a game-changer, a digital alchemist turning browsing behaviors into gold, transforming casual visitors into loyal customers, and elevating the shopping experience into a realm of almost magical personalization. So, unleash AI on your e-commerce platforms and watch as mundane transactions transform into extraordinary experiences, and your sales, much like the ambitions of every AI-equipped e-commerce mogul, reach for the stars.

In the grand casino of commerce, where entrepreneurs roll the dice daily on decisions big and small, AI-driven analytics serves as the card-counting whiz kid, whispering in

your ear which bets might pay off and which are as promising as a snowball in a sauna. This isn't just about crunching numbers; it's about turning those numbers into narratives, weaving them into strategies, and transforming raw data into the gold dust that paves the path to profitability.

Imagine you're the captain of a ship called Enterprise in the vast ocean of the market. Your AI analytics is like having an omniscient navigator aboard, one who can read not only the stars but also the depths of the ocean. It tells you where the currents are favorable, where storms might brew, and where the treasure islands of untapped market potential lie hidden under waves of data.

In the dynamic realm of marketing, AI-driven analytics transforms vast seas of consumer data into precise maps of market trends and customer preferences. It's like having a spyglass that shows not just the horizon but also what every distant ship is carrying and where it's headed. This intelligence allows businesses to tailor their marketing strategies with surgical precision—targeting the right demographic with the right message at the right time,

dramatically increasing the effectiveness of advertising campaigns and boosting ROI as if by magic.

In the intricate world of supply chain management, AI analytics acts as the grandmaster of logistics, foreseeing disruptions before they cause havoc. It examines patterns from historical data to predict future bottlenecks, suggests optimal inventory levels, and even recommends the best suppliers based on past performance, price changes, and delivery timeliness. It's akin to playing chess with a supercomputer—you're always five moves ahead, and your operations run as smoothly as a well-oiled locomotive, even when the tracks twist unexpectedly.

Financial forecasting under the guidance of AI becomes less a game of guesswork and more a science. AI models can pore over years of financial data to identify trends, predict future revenues, and warn of potential downturns before they manifest. It's like having a financial fortune teller in your boardroom, one whose crystal ball is an algorithm sophisticated enough to make Nostradamus green with envy.

And let's not overlook customer service, where AI analytics can predict and preempt issues before they

escalate into crises. By analyzing customer interaction data, AI can identify patterns that may lead to dissatisfaction and churn. It proactively addresses these issues, perhaps by suggesting changes to service protocols or by initiating targeted customer outreach. It's customer service not just with a smile, but with a premonition of your needs before you even know them yourself.

Integrate AI analytics into all major decision-making processes. Let it be your guide in marketing, supply chain management, financial planning, and customer service.

Use AI-driven insights to personalize customer interactions. Tailor your communications and offerings to meet the unique preferences and needs of each customer segment.

Leverage predictive analytics to stay ahead of market trends. Use AI to not only react to the current market environment but to forecast future changes and adapt proactively.

Automate routine data analysis tasks, freeing up your human talent to focus on creative and strategic pursuits that AI cannot replicate.

Can Artificial Intelligence Really Help Me Make Money? Here Is How

Continuously train and retrain your AI models on the latest data. AI analytics is only as good as the information it feeds on, so keep it nourished with fresh, relevant data.

By integrating AI-driven analytics into your business toolkit, you transform from a mere player in the market to a formidable strategist, navigating the complex currents of commerce with a prescience that could define the future of your enterprise. It's not just about making smarter decisions; it's about making visionary ones, where each step is informed, intentional, and ingeniously inspired by the deep insights only AI can provide.

Imagine the scene: a bustling business landscape, each company a busy beehive of activity. In this hive, human workers buzz from task to task, a symphony of productivity — that is until the drones of redundancy and inefficiency swarm in. Enter AI, the swatter of unnecessary costs and the oiler of creaky operational gears. This isn't just your average, garden-variety automation; it's like having a wizard in the wings, capable of transforming clunky, old-school processes into sleek, streamlined operations with a flick of its algorithmic wand.

Can Artificial Intelligence Really Help Me Make Money? Here Is How

Think of AI as the Mary Poppins of the business world; just as she flies in with her umbrella to fix family dysfunctions, AI parachutes into businesses to tidy up processes with a touch that's as magical as it is methodical. It sweeps through the data, finds patterns that no human eye could ever detect, and automates tasks that are so mundane they could make an insomniac snooze.

In customer service, AI introduces chatbots, those tirelessly cheery digital conversationalists that handle customer inquiries 24/7. They don't need coffee breaks, they don't get grumpy, and they certainly don't ask for overtime pay. It's like having an army of customer service agents who are always in a good mood, even if they're asked the same question a thousand times. The result? Reduced staffing costs, quicker response times, and happier customers who aren't left listening to the dreaded hold music.

In the realm of accounting, AI becomes the bean counter supreme. It can sift through expenses, automate invoicing, and ensure every digit is in its rightful place with the precision of a Swiss watchmaker. Gone are the days of human errors that could lead to financial faux pas; AI catches every misplaced decimal, every accidental

oversight. It's like having an eagle-eyed accountant who can spot a financial misstep from a mile away, all without breaking a sweat.

Then there's inventory management, where AI transforms into the ultimate organizer. It predicts stock needs based on real-time data, manages orders, and even suggests discounts for overstock items. It's as if you've employed a psychic warehouse manager who can foresee sales trends before they happen. This AI doesn't just manage your stock; it anticipates it, ensuring you never run out of bestsellers while also avoiding the graveyard of unsold items.

For the forward-thinking entrepreneur ready to harness the power of AI for automation, here are some strategic maneuvers to consider:

Implement AI-driven tools in high-volume, repetitive task areas. Whether it's customer queries, payroll, or inventory, let AI handle the grunt work, freeing up your human talent for more complex, creative tasks.

Monitor and analyze AI performance continuously. Just because it's automated doesn't mean it's set in stone.

Regular audits ensure your AI systems remain efficient and effective.

Scale AI solutions as you grow. Start small with one process, measure the impact, and then expand AI deployment across other areas of your business as you witness the benefits.

Educate and train your workforce to work alongside AI. Automation isn't about replacing jobs; it's about augmenting them. Ensure your team understands how to leverage AI tools to make their jobs easier and more productive.

Stay updated on the latest AI advancements. The field of AI is evolving rapidly. Keeping abreast of new technologies ensures you can continually enhance your automation strategies.

By integrating AI into your business operations, you're not just cutting costs; you're catapulting your company into a new era of efficiency and productivity. It's about turning the mundane into the magnificent, transforming everyday operations with a touch of tech wizardry that not only saves money but also sprinkles a little magic along the way. So, let AI take the wheel of routine tasks, and watch as your

business accelerates towards a future where cost-saving is just the beginning.

In the grand theatrical production that is modern commerce, where every customer interaction can swing the pendulum of profit, AI steps onto the stage as the virtuoso of customer service, ready to transform the mundane monologue of traditional support into a captivating dialogue of efficiency and personalization. Picture this: a world where AI isn't just an actor in the wings but the star of the show, delivering a performance so nuanced and tailored that customers can hardly believe the service isn't human-powered.

Visualize a typical day in the not-so-distant future, in a bustling call center now quietly humming with the sound of AI at work. Here, chatbots, those tireless digital darlings, handle inquiries with the dexterity of a seasoned concierge. They're fluent in all languages, from English to Emoji, and can toggle between them with the ease of a linguistic gymnast. No query too complex, no complaint too convoluted; these AI assistants parse customer emotions and context faster than a teenager texts at a traffic light.

But the magic of AI in customer service isn't confined to text on a screen. Enter voice recognition technology, where AI transforms into an auditory oracle, understanding tones, accents, and even the subtlest nuances of speech. It's as if every customer support agent has suddenly acquired the ear of a UN interpreter, but with the added ability to instantly recall every interaction, every preference, and every past purchase of the caller.

Imagine further, the AI-enhanced video support services, where facial recognition and mood analysis technology allow virtual agents to not only respond to queries but to anticipate customer needs based on visual cues. It's as though the AI has developed empathy, providing comfort with a soothing word or a timely joke, turning frustrating service calls into exchanges as pleasant as a chat over coffee.

Beyond reacting, AI in customer service proactively engages customers based on their behavior patterns and purchasing history. It recommends products, reminds them of replenishments, and even suggests custom promotions that feel personally crafted just for them. It's like having a personal shopper for every customer, one who remembers

that you prefer your gadgets in black, detest late deliveries, and celebrate your cat's birthday with the purchase of a new toy each year.

For entrepreneurs looking to ride the crest of this AI wave in customer service, here are several strategic steps to consider:

Invest in AI systems that integrate seamlessly with your existing CRM tools, ensuring a smooth transition and immediate uptake in efficiency.

Train your AI meticulously, feeding it vast amounts of interaction data, so that its learning curve skyrockets, making it as knowledgeable as your best customer service representative.

Focus on personalization; use AI to tailor interactions to individual customer preferences, making each interaction feel special and understood.

Ensure transparency and maintain an option for human intervention. Customers should know when they are speaking to AI and easily switch to a human agent if desired — blending high tech with high touch.

Regularly update and maintain your AI systems to handle new queries and scenarios as your market evolves,

ensuring that the quality of service grows along with your business.

By integrating AI into your customer service operations, you're not just keeping up with the times; you're setting the pace, providing a level of service that is as delightfully surprising as it is undeniably efficient. In this AI-augmented future, customer service becomes less of a cost center and more of a loyalty builder, turning every call, chat, or email into an opportunity to impress, engage, and retain. This isn't just about answering questions; it's about anticipating needs, exceeding expectations, and building relationships that last. So let AI take the wheel, and watch as your customer service ratings—and your profits—soar.

Chapter 10: Preparing for an AI-Driven Future

As we teeter on the cusp of the AI revolution, preparing oneself for this technological transformation isn't just wise; it's akin to strapping on a jetpack before jumping off the cliff of outdated practices into the exhilarating abyss of the future. You're not just learning; you're launching into a new paradigm where knowledge isn't just power; it's profit.

Imagine your brain as a dusty attic, filled with the cobwebs of conventional wisdom and the musty smell of antiquated ideas. The first step in preparing for the AI-driven future is to fling open the windows, let in the fresh air of cutting-edge knowledge, and start rearranging the furniture. This isn't your grandma's attic anymore; it's the command center of your future empire.

Start by plunging headfirst into the ocean of AI education. This means not just paddling in the shallow waters of popular science articles but diving deep into the Marianas Trench of AI knowledge. Take online courses— many of which are as free as birds and just as liberating—

offered by prestigious universities that won't just teach you AI; they'll immerse you in it. Coursera, edX, and Udacity become your new Netflix, binge-watching machine learning, neural networks, and robotics.

But why stop at virtual learning? The world is your educational oyster, ripe for the plucking. Attend AI conferences, workshops, and seminars. Rub elbows with the Einsteins and Edisons of the AI world, where networking does not involve routers and cables but handshakes and business cards. These events are like live concerts compared to listening to recordings; the vibe is infectious, and the learning is electric.

And don't forget the treasure troves of knowledge contained in books, your reading list should look like the who's who of AI scholarship. Treat these books like sacred texts, poring over them not just to glean information but to question, critique, and engage with the material. It's not just reading; it's a dialogue with the authors.

Equally important is practical experience. Dive into AI projects. Use platforms like Kaggle to test your skills or GitHub to contribute to open-source AI projects. It's like

joining the gym for your brain, but instead of lifting weights, you're lifting datasets and algorithms.

Curate your curriculum. Mix online courses with physical workshops. Blend reading with real-world experimentation.

Stay updated on AI trends. Subscribe to AI newsletters, follow key AI influencers on social media, and set Google alerts for AI breakthroughs.

Network aggressively. Connect with AI professionals and thought leaders online. LinkedIn can be your digital salon where ideas and opportunities mingle over virtual coffee.

Apply your knowledge. Work on AI projects, either independently or in collaboration. Nothing cements knowledge like application.

Reflect and revise. Regularly assess what you've learned and how you can apply it. This reflection is the polish that turns raw knowledge into market-ready skills.

By transforming yourself into a veritable AI aficionado, you're not just preparing to survive in an AI-driven future; you're gearing up to thrive, lead, and profit. This isn't just an education; it's an evolution. So, strap on your learning cap

and prepare to ride the exhilarating wave of AI—it promises a thrilling adventure in both knowledge and wealth.

Embarking upon the high seas of the AI ecosystem without a compass of networking is akin to steering a rudderless ship—exciting yet potentially fruitless. In the vast, interconnected world of artificial intelligence, where data streams flow faster than gossip in a small town, weaving a web of strategic relationships isn't just beneficial; it's crucial to survival and success. This networking isn't your average schmoozing at stuffy cocktail parties; it's an exhilarating expedition into the heart of innovation, where every handshake and exchanged business card can lead to opportunities as boundless as the digital realms AI inhabits.

Imagine diving into a digital melting pot where tech titans, quirky coders, and visionary venture capitalists mingle. Here, online forums, social media platforms, and AI conferences serve as the bustling marketplaces of ideas and influence. Platforms like LinkedIn, Twitter, and even niche online communities such as GitHub or Stack Exchange become your playgrounds. Engaging here is like launching tweets that are part homing pigeons, part

fireworks—designed to dazzle and direct attention right back to your burgeoning brand.

But why stop at virtual connections when the physical world offers just as much bounty? AI conferences and workshops are the watering holes where the big beasts of the tech world come to drink. Events like the Neural Information Processing Systems Conference (NeurIPS) or the International Conference on Machine Learning (ICML) are not just gatherings; they're galas of the mind, where the air crackles with ideas and the potential for partnerships permeates every conversation. Here, a casual coffee break can brew a business deal, and a serendipitous seating arrangement at a keynote speech can seed the next big startup.

In these high-energy hubs, the aim is to be both seen and heard. Deliver a presentation, pose a poignant question, or release a paper on recent AI innovations. Each action is like sending out a flare over dark waters, signaling your location and expertise to fellow voyagers in the AI arena. However, building a network is akin to planting a garden—it requires more than scattering seeds to the wind. You must tend it with the care of a devoted gardener. Follow up on

those conference connections, engage regularly with your social media contacts, contribute thoughtfully to online discussions. It's about nurturing these relationships with the same precision and dedication that AI applies to optimizing algorithms.

Create a robust online presence. Regularly update your professional profiles, publish articles, and share insights that reflect your expertise and passion for AI.

Be a giver, not just a taker. Offer advice, make introductions, share resources without immediate expectations. The ecosystem thrives on reciprocity.

Target your networking. Identify leaders in specific AI niches you're interested in and reach out with personalized communication. It's about quality, not just quantity.

Leverage local meetups and tech talks. Sometimes the most valuable connections are right in your backyard. Local events can be less overwhelming and offer more immediate engagement opportunities.

Stay consistent and patient. Building a meaningful network takes time. Consistent effort is like watering that garden; do it well, and it will bloom.

Can Artificial Intelligence Really Help Me Make Money? Here Is How

By mastering the art of networking within the AI community, you're not just building a list of contacts; you're crafting a mosaic of potential mentors, partners, and friends who can propel your AI endeavors from mere concepts to lucrative realities. In this networked age, your net worth truly does hinge on your network. So cast wide, dive deep, and watch as the connections you cultivate today turn into the capital of tomorrow.

In the rapidly evolving realm of artificial intelligence, resting on your laurels is akin to sitting on a conveyor belt moving backward—rather comical to onlookers but hardly productive. Staying ahead in AI is not just about sprinting ahead of the competition; it's about maintaining a pace that allows continuous absorption, application, and adaptation of new knowledge. Think of it as being on a treadmill set on a gentle incline, perpetually pushing you to step up your game, except this treadmill comes with an endless stream of data, algorithms, and technologies that you must juggle while jogging.

Consider the unrelenting pace of AI advancements; to merely keep pace can be dizzying, yet exhilarating. Continuous learning in AI is less about catching up and

more about tuning into a rhythm that keeps your skills, knowledge, and strategies in harmony with technological progress. This learning isn't confined to the rigors of formal education but is a vibrant, ongoing process that happens on job boards, in online forums, through digital courses, and during sleepless nights spent experimenting with code.

To weave this continuous learning into the very fabric of your professional life, start by treating every project, every task, and indeed, every failure, as a learning opportunity. Did your neural network model spit out predictions that were less accurate than a weather forecast? Fantastic! Each misstep is a puzzle piece, revealing a bit more about the intricate picture of AI's capabilities and limitations.

Further, immerse yourself in the ocean of Massive Open Online Courses (MOOCs), webinars, and specialized workshops that delve into everything from basic machine learning concepts to advanced AI applications in quantum computing. Platforms like Coursera, Udacity, or MIT OpenCourseWare offer not just courses but gateways to new dimensions of understanding, each module a portal to potential mastery.

Can Artificial Intelligence Really Help Me Make Money? Here Is How

And don't overlook the value of peer interaction. The AI community is vibrantly alive with forums like Stack Overflow, Reddit, or specific LinkedIn groups where warriors of the AI frontier gather to exchange knowledge, solve problems, and share a meme or two. Engaging here is like joining a roundtable of knights, each armed with the swords of syntax and shields of algorithms, battling the dragons of bugs and errors.

Set regular learning goals. Whether it's mastering a new programming language every year or diving into a new AI sub-field, keep setting the educational bar higher.

Participate in hackathons and coding challenges. These are not just competitions but crucibles in which skills are both tested and tempered.

Teach what you learn. Whether through blogs, YouTube tutorials, or local meetups, teaching is a method of learning that cements knowledge and expands understanding.

Subscribe to AI research journals and publications. Keeping abreast of the latest research ensures you're as updated as the morning news.

Can Artificial Intelligence Really Help Me Make Money? Here Is How

Apply your learning to real-world problems. Theoretical knowledge is a golden key, but its true value is realized when it unlocks practical challenges.

Embrace the philosophy that in the world of AI, learning is not a task or a checkpoint but a continual journey—a thrilling expedition where each discovery propels you not just towards professional success but towards becoming a pioneer on the AI frontier. So, lace up your boots, adjust your compass, and prepare for a trek where the path is strewn with data, the landscapes are complex algorithms, and the horizons are limitless possibilities. In this AI-driven adventure, the treasure isn't just the knowledge gained along the way but the myriad ways it can be harnessed to fill your coffers to the brim.

In the grand chess game of modern business, where AI is your queen, sweeping across the board with formidable power, ethical usage isn't just a rule; it's a strategy that can safeguard your kingdom against revolt and ruin. Imagine AI ethics not as a leash but as a laser-guided navigation system, steering your business ventures through murky waters, where the monsters of misuse and the pirates of privacy breaches lurk.

Can Artificial Intelligence Really Help Me Make Money? Here Is How

To wield AI ethically is to command a ship with not just speed but a compass, ensuring that your technological prowess is matched by your moral compass. This approach isn't merely about avoiding scandal or sidestepping legal battles—though it does both admirably—it's about building a fortress of trust with your customers, a commodity more valuable than the slickest AI algorithm or the most comprehensive data set.

First, consider transparency, the bedrock of ethical AI. This isn't just about opening the kimono a bit to show you're wearing shorts; it's about showing all the gears, bolts, and inner workings of your AI operations. When your AI decides who gets a loan or what news gets shown, can you explain 'how' and 'why' to a layperson? If your AI were on trial, could it explain its decision-making process to a jury of its users? Ensuring your AI's actions are as clear as a bell not only builds trust but also demystifies AI technology, turning fear of the unknown into awe of what's known.

Next up is the principle of fairness, ensuring your AI doesn't play favorites or indulge in digital discrimination. This means regular audits for bias—because AI, like a dutiful mirror, reflects both the best and the worst of what it's

shown. Regularly scrutinizing your data and algorithms for bias ensures that your AI treats all users with impartiality, not because it has a heart, but because you programmed it to be fair. Imagine your AI as a judge who must decide without prejudice—blindfolded to bias, attentive only to the balance of data.

Privacy, the crown jewel of ethical AI, involves handling personal data with the care of a jeweler clutching a diamond. It's about collecting only what you need, using it only as agreed, and safeguarding it as if it were your own. In an age where data breaches are more common than colds, protecting user data isn't just good ethics; it's good business.

Now, accountability: AI may make decisions, but remember, it's you who'll be held responsible. Establishing clear protocols for when things go wrong—because occasionally they will—is vital. Have a plan, have a process, have a person whose job it is to handle the fallout. It's like having both a lifeboat and a lifejacket under your seat—the hope is you'll never need them, but you'll thank the stars they're there if you do.

Develop and enforce a rigorous AI ethics policy. Make it as common as the coffee machine—used daily, appreciated by everyone.

Engage with stakeholders, from customers to employees, in the AI development process. Their insights can help identify potential ethical pitfalls you might miss.

Educate your team on the importance of AI ethics. They're your first line of defense against unethical AI usage.

Regularly audit and update your AI systems. Check not just for performance but for principles.

Be transparent with users about how AI is used in your products or services. An informed user is an empowered user.

By championing ethical practices in AI, you're not just adhering to best practices; you're setting the standard, distinguishing your business as a beacon of integrity in a sea of opportunism. This is how you turn the cutting-edge tool of AI into a trusted ally that not only earns money but also earns respect. And in the bustling market of tomorrow, respect is a currency that's always in demand.

Imagine, if you will, a future not too distant, where AI has woven itself into the very fabric of society like some sort

of digital deity. This isn't just a future where your fridge orders your milk (because it knows you're about to run out, thanks to the sneaky midnight cereal habits) or your car negotiates rush hour traffic (while you nap). No, we're peering deeper, into a societal transformation so profound, it makes the invention of the wheel seem like a minor tweak.

In this futuristic spectacle, AI in healthcare goes beyond suggesting you take an aspirin. Imagine AI systems so adept that they predict illnesses before you even think to sneeze, deploying nanobots to fix your cells so you can skip the doctor and head straight to your salsa class. Health AI could extend lifespans, turning the daunting concept of a mid-life crisis into a tri-quarter-life crisis because you've now got three times as long to figure it all out.

Now, cast your gaze upon the financial markets, those wild beasts of civilization where fortunes are made and lost in less time than it takes to say "stock market crash." AI here becomes the ultimate oracle, not just predicting market shifts but actively balancing them, preventing the financial apocalypses that keep Wall Street awake at night. It's like having a financial superhero who's half Warren Buffett, half

Can Artificial Intelligence Really Help Me Make Money?
Here Is How

Tony Stark, managing economic stability with a mix of market savvy and metallic prowess.

Let's not sidestep the societal challenges, though. With AI taking over tasks from truck driving to legal analysis, the job landscape isn't just changing; it's evolving. While some cry doomsday over lost jobs, envision instead a world where humans are freed from drudgery to pursue careers in innovation, creativity, and personal fulfillment. It's not about jobs lost but lives gained. Schools might teach creativity and critical thinking over calculus, and your job could be as a virtual reality adventure designer or a robot personality programmer.

But, what about ethics and privacy? Here's where it gets spicy. AI's ability to process data could lead to a surveillance state that makes "Big Brother" look like an amateur, or it could usher in an era of unparalleled personal freedom, where crime is predicted and prevented before you can say "Minority Report." The key is in wielding this power wisely. Society might need to develop an AI ethics constitution, debated in forums more heated than a reality TV show finale.

Can Artificial Intelligence Really Help Me Make Money? Here Is How

Stay educated and adaptable. The future belongs to those who can pivot, not those stuck lamenting over lost opportunities. Be the pivoter, not the pivotee.

Invest in AI literacy. Whether you're a coder or a candlestick maker, knowing your AI from your elbow will be key.

Influence AI development through advocacy and public discourse. Get involved in shaping how AI evolves in governance and policy. Voting on AI laws might become as common as jury duty.

Prepare for new career opportunities. Future-proof your career by focusing on skills that AI can't replicate easily—yet. Think empathy, creativity, and interpersonal dynamics.

Promote and practice ethical AI usage. Be the role model for how AI should be integrated into society, not a cautionary tale.

So, buckle up and enjoy the ride into this AI-driven future. It promises to be as thrilling as surfing on rocket boosters, and with the right preparation, you'll not only witness history—you'll make it. And maybe, just maybe, you'll make a fortune while you're at it.

Conclusion

And so, we reach the grand denouement of our thrilling tome, a saga as rich in insights as it is in anticipation of a future sculpted by the deft hands of AI. In the vast and verdant gardens of human endeavor, where the seeds of technology have germinated into structures of startling complexity and capability, AI stands as a towering oak, its branches stretching into every conceivable industry, from the chaotic trading floors of finance to the serene rows of agricultural greenery.

Reflect upon the odyssey we have embarked upon, from the primal stirrings of AI in the financial sector to the lofty integration of AI with quantum computing and robotics, each chapter a stepping stone towards mastering this behemoth of binary intellect. Our journey was not merely about understanding AI but about harnessing its potent potential to fuel our entrepreneurial quests and line our coffers with the gold of innovation and efficiency.

Armed now with the acumen to navigate the AI landscape—from the boardrooms bedecked with screens displaying market trends predicted by AI, to the startup

garages where robots and algorithms are being tweaked to perform with sublime efficiency—we see the horizon of possibility expand exponentially. As we stand, like captains at the helm of our ships, gazing towards this horizon, it is clear: the future is not just coming; it has arrived, and it is coded.

We chuckled at the thought of AI as a meticulous bean counter in accounting, and smirked at the image of digital concierges catering to our every whim in the retail space, all the while preparing ourselves for the ethical quandaries that this new digital workforce brings to bear. We danced through dialogues on networking within the pulsing heart of the AI community, where every interaction could be the spark that ignites the next groundbreaking venture. We ventured into the thicket of continual learning, knowing full well that in the realm of AI, stagnation is tantamount to regression.

In this climactic cascade of knowledge and narrative, remember that each piece of advice, each strategy unveiled, and each precautionary tale spun is a gear in the grand mechanism of your future success. It's a toolkit, rich with the cogs and wheels of wisdom that, when applied, will not only

keep you abreast of AI advancements but propel you ahead of the curve.

So as you close this book, let not your journey end here. Let the conclusion of each chapter be the genesis of your own exploration into how AI can not only augment your current operations but revolutionize them. Experiment boldly, implement strategically, and engage ethically. And above all, remember that in the theatre of business and technology, you are both audience and playwright, spectator and star, as you script your own path through the AI revolution.

May your enterprises flourish, your intellect expand, and your coffers overflow as you wield the formidable power of AI. From concept to cash, from binary to billions, let this book be your beacon as you navigate the exciting, lucrative waters of an AI-driven future. And never forget—amidst the algorithms and analytics, keep your wit sharp and your humor sharper, for in the world of artificial intelligence, it is the most human traits that will ensure not just survival, but triumph.

Please Leave a Review

Did this book tickle your techy taste buds and boost your money-making brainpower? If you had a blast flipping through these chapters and found the golden nuggets of financial wisdom you were after, I have a tiny favor to ask.

Imagine the joy of countless readers, just like you, discovering this gem thanks to your rave review. You'll be a hero, a guiding star in their quest for AI money-making enlightenment! Plus, think of all the good karma points you'll rack up (the financial type, of course).

So, if you're feeling the love, click this review link (or point your phone camera to this QR code) and let the world know how this book rocked your world (and bank account). I (and future readers) will thank you from the bottom of our silicon hearts!

Click Here to Leave Review

www.ingramcontent.com/pod-product-compliance
Lightning Source LLC
Chambersburg PA
CBHW062352220526
45472CB00008B/1776